Prayer

THAT'S
Caught *and* Taught

MENTORING THE NEXT GENERATION

CAROL MADISON

PRAYERSHOP
PUBLISHING
Terre Haute, IN

PrayerShop Publishing is the publishing arm of the National Day of Prayer Task Force. Centered on the Lord Jesus Christ, the National Day of Prayer Task Force exists to mobilize unified public prayer for America. PrayerShop produces both resources that disciple people at all levels of prayer and that help churches make prayer more foundational to their ministries. Its online prayer store, prayershop.org, has more than 150 prayer resources available for purchase.

© 2019 Carol Madison

ISBN (Print): 978-1-935012-84-9
ISBN (E-Book): 978-1-935012-85-6

PrayerShop Publishing
P.O. Box 10667
Terre Haute, IN 47801

1 2 3 4 5 | 2023 2022 2021 2020 2019

Acknowledgements

I can't possibly list all the people who have spoken into my prayer life. I've gleaned many insights from participation in countless prayer groups with powerful and experienced intercessors. Some of you scared me, but you taught me new ways to pray!

I'm also grateful for many wonderful national prayer leaders who graciously model prayer practices that challenge and refresh me. And I'm so thankful for my friends who practice prayer with me in small groups, on the phone, one-on-one, and in the prayer room at my church. We've enjoyed learning together.

I couldn't have written a book on prayer mentoring without the practical experiences and patience offered by my prayer mentor groups at Hillside Church. You listened, questioned, discussed, laughed, and encouraged me as I developed our mentoring curriculum. You endeared yourselves to me as friends. For that reason, you get your names in a book: Amy, Becky, Carolyn, Celeste, Danielle, Elaine, Gabi, Heather G., Heather T., Heather W., Heidi, Hillary, Jaeda, Jen, Jenna, Kasey, Katie, Kay, Kelsey, Kim, Kristen, Leah, Lindsay, Linsey, Mai, Megan, Nikki, Susanna, Suzanne, and Tara.

So many dear friends and family members prayed me through this project. I can't express how blessed I am. A shout-out goes to my Bible Study Fellowship group leader, Heidi, who both prayed and held me accountable. I wrote nearly every Saturday for five months because I knew you would ask me about it on Tuesday.

Many of you suggested I write a book on prayer mentoring, but I resisted for quite some time. I finally listened when Kari told me over a cup of coffee that she believed the Lord wanted me to do this—and then Jon Graf, my publisher, confirmed it by inviting me to submit a manuscript. Thank you to everyone who encouraged me.

I especially thank my dad and mom, who not only prayed for me and demonstrated prayer in our home, but also took me to weekly prayer services during my younger years. I learned at an early age how to pray corporately and belong to a church that values prayer. Several times you did not make it to my high school basketball, volleyball, or softball games because you instead attended a prayer meeting. I never resented that or thought it unusual. You just modeled prayer as a Kingdom priority.

Most of all, my thanks to Jesus for personally mentoring and praying alongside me, especially during late nights and desperate times. When I called, You answered. It's true, Jesus. You change *everything*. Even me.

– Carol Madison

Contents

Introduction

CRAWLING UNDER THE STAGE TO PRAY

I drove three hours with my nephew Brad to a campus outreach at a university in a neighboring state, sponsored by a ministry focused on reaching the next generation and awakening our culture to Jesus.

I wasn't sure what to expect, but I readied myself with ear plugs. One of the event leaders recruited Brad and me to provide intercessory prayer backstage while well-known bands played and students from this secular university packed the arena. Midway through the event, Nick, a young millennial evangelist, planned to preach the gospel to thousands of students drawn by the concert atmosphere.

With ear plugs secure and my heart pounding from the loud beat of the music, I received my assignment.

"When Nick gets up to preach, we want you to crawl under the stage to pray," said Steph, the young staff member directing backstage prayer.

"What? Are you kidding?" I asked.

Do you know how old I am? I thought. I couldn't picture crawling on my hands and knees to situate myself directly under center stage.

Steph was serious, and a short time later Brad and I crawled toward our assignment. We crouched there through the throbbing music above us. Then we prayed when Nick took the stage and started preaching.

At first the crowd acted restless, milling about and talking. But we prayed fervently. Suddenly, as Nick reached the core of the gospel message, the crowd miraculously hushed and listened. I say miraculously because the Holy Spirit clearly worked. Hundreds of students reset their lives to Jesus that night.

And I've crawled under stages ever since.

TIME TO INVEST

The saying, "prayer is better caught than taught," doesn't quite apply to a mentoring relationship. Your prayer life is a powerful example to others, and people can catch that passion for prayer from you. But intentional teaching of prayer principles equips others to embrace a full and enriching prayer life. Prayer needs to be both caught *and* taught.

This book focuses on serving the next generation. It's about taking all the prayer experiences God has given you over your lifetime of walking with Jesus—and passing those biblical truths and prayer practices on to those who follow you in the faith.

It's also about hoping for the future. When we mentor others, we invest in future generations. Others invested in us and we, in turn, can strategically share the riches of faith we've acquired over the years. Psalm 78:4 speaks of our responsibility to "tell the next generation the praiseworthy deeds of the LORD, his power, and the wonders he has done."

In these pages, I hope to encourage you to mentor the next generation in prayer. I offer many of the lessons I've taught as a prayer mentor. You can use these lessons, add your own experiences and insights, and adapt the handouts in the back. You'll also find a journal to write about your answers to prayer or to share God's workings in your life. When the God of the universe moves on your behalf, you need to write it down! Remember to remember, and share those stories with others.

Take a step of faith and mentor others. Invite the Spirit to direct you as you read and study the prayer principles in this book. God looks more for a willing heart than a person seasoned with years of prayer. Now is your time to invest in others, teaching them the power of intercession and other aspects of prayer.

There will come a day when I can no longer crawl on the hard floor under a stage. But I want to look back and see that the fervency and hope in prayer carries on—with or without me.

I want the next generation of intercessors to join me *now*, under the stage.

CHAPTER 1

Answering a Heart-Racing Call

A t that moment, I knew the Lord spoke to me. I felt a flush of emotion and a bit of heart-racing. I could not concentrate on the dialogue around me. Something stirred within.

I had just previewed the movie *War Room* with members of America's National Prayer Committee. The movie tells the powerful story of an older woman intentionally investing in the life of a younger woman by mentoring her in prayer. One of the producers of the movie joined us for a question-and-answer session and to hear our feedback. But I barely joined in the conversation because my mind filled with conviction from the Holy Spirit.

Then I heard that quiet voice in my thoughts. It's a voice I recognize. *What are you doing to mentor the next generation in prayer?*

I silently prayed my answer to the Lord. *I don't know what this means, but I'm willing. You're going to have to show me because I have no idea how to do this.*

Over the next week or so, I continued to pray about it. I gained no clear direction until another thought impressed on me, presumably from the Lord again. *Six women for six months.*

HERE WE GO!

I kept pondering and praying. Six women for six months. That's all I knew.

A couple of weeks later, I walked through the lobby of my church and greeted two young women sitting and chatting with each other.

"Hey, Carol," one of them said. "We were just talking about you. We were wondering if you would ever mentor us."

I like it when God is direct with me.

I invited them to find four other women willing to meet for six months so I could mentor them in prayer. My criteria: they needed to be younger than me, and willing to explore new insights and approaches to their prayer lives.

Suddenly, six enthusiastic young women signed up, eager to embark on an unknown journey. Without a curriculum, I created session-by-session lessons based on my personal experiences, a lifetime of learning, and key biblical principles. After every lesson, I prayed about the next topic the Lord wanted me to teach. Month after month, I kept adding to the curriculum, one lesson at a time.

We met twice a month. I assigned each participant a prayer partner. Then we switched up every two months, so they could enjoy partnering with three different women. I assigned the women to meet with their prayer partners in between our sessions to discuss what we just learned, and then pray together.

In those six months, I completed 12 lessons I could use with future groups. But more rewarding than that, I had six new friends who continued practicing the prayer principles in their personal lives, with their families, and in our church.

So far, I have mentored 30 young women in my church for six months each, with a list of potential participants who want to join a future session. As the prayer ministries director of my church, I take on a variety of responsibilities and opportunities to encourage a prayer movement. But mentoring the next generation remains one of my greatest investments.

HANGING BY A THREAD

Of course, there are few experts on prayer. Mostly, it's just people on a journey who learn through triumph and tragedy to plunge deeper in their dependency upon God through prayer. The more one practices prayer, the more the Holy Spirit reveals both the joy and power of this lifestyle. And sometimes it's not so much about your knowledge of prayer that you pass on, but more about the hope you convey.

The day before a recent Thanksgiving, I received a thank-you note in the mail from a woman who attended a women's retreat I spoke at a few years earlier. I did not recognize her name, but I noted her address from my hometown. She simply thanked me for encouraging her not to give up and to continue praying with hope. She shared some Scripture, but no other details.

The next day, I enjoyed an evening meal with my mom, aunt, and uncle at a local restaurant. We discovered that not many places stayed open on Thanksgiving night, so we ended up in a popular chain restaurant better known for breakfast and pie than turkey and all the fixings.

I noticed a couple seated next to us, and after a moment the woman approached our table.

"Are you Carol Madison?" she asked. She introduced herself and explained, "I sent you a note recently."

Okay, what are the chances of sitting next to the thank-you-note writer at the only restaurant open on Thanksgiving Day? Well, with God they proved quite good!

The woman filled in the back story about why she wrote the note. At the time of the retreat, she'd given up on her adult son gaining victory over his drug addiction. She reminded me I prayed with her at the end of a session. That encouragement kept the woman praying with hope for her son.

Now, three years later, she told me the rest of her story. Her son gave his life to Jesus, grew in faith, and gained freedom from his drug addiction. Even more, he would soon graduate from a year-long treatment program in a well-known Christian drug rehabilitation program.

I didn't know it at the time, but at the retreat, this mom hung on by a thread. She needed someone to share with her the power of prayer, the hope in Christ, and a vision for her son's future. It renewed and re-energized her prayer life on behalf of her son, and God broke through powerfully when she determined not to give up.

Sometimes mentoring simply means demonstrating hope and faith in a God who answers prayer.

TELLING YOUR STORIES

You might feel unqualified to mentor another person in prayer. Many of us do. But you have a story. You have watched God work through faithfulness and fervency in prayer. You have life experiences and examples of answered prayer. Perhaps this book can offer tools and resources that will encourage you to take a step of faith to begin mentoring others.

More importantly, you need to share your stories. In this book, I include many of my stories about God's glorious work through prayer. But I encourage you to write out your own stories. You don't need to present only the profound. You don't need to carefully craft them. You can keep them simple. Just convey hope. Hope in the God who performs breakthroughs and miracles on behalf of His people, and awaits invitations to do more. He wants you to ask Him for your needs and for the seemingly impossible. He's also waiting for you to share your prayer life with the next generation.

START TO PRAY NOW

God can place you in situations to mentor the next generation. It doesn't matter your age or theirs; a generation always follows behind you. As a parent, your children need your stories for encouragement to pray with greater faith. As a grandparent, God gives you a unique opportunity to influence generations long after you leave this earth. And if you are like me—a lifelong single person with no children—you still can inspire others to believe in and trust a powerful, miracle-working God.

Whether you realize it or not, others pay attention to how you pray and trust God. Ask God to expand your vision. Pray to become a Romans 15:13 conveyor of hope in prayer:

> May the God of hope fill you with all joy and peace as you trust in him, so that you may overflow with hope by the power of the Holy Spirit.

Prepare to share. Start writing down your stories of answered prayer and the truths God showed you through personal life lessons. If God answered a prayer, you gained a story. Someone needs to hear it. Someone needs encouragement to pray with greater faith.

Someone needs *you* as a mentor.

THINK ABOUT IT

These questions and activities can help prepare you for mentoring others in prayer.

1. What is the most significant answer to prayer you can recall from your lifetime? Jot it down.
2. Ask the Lord to prompt your memory about other personal stories of answered prayer. Keep adding to your list as you read this book.

In the back of the book, use the journal to list stories for future use.

3. List potential people you could mentor in prayer. Keep adding to the list as God brings people to mind. Pray over your list, asking God to expand it. Invite Him to pinpoint the right people and the right time to launch a mentoring relationship.

PRAYER RESPONSE

Spending time in prayer can also prepare you for mentoring. Honestly tell God how you feel about fulfilling this role.

1. Do you feel inadequate to mentor others? Write a prayer inviting God to expand your vision, give you courage, and prepare you to mentor others.
2. Pray God will use you to mentor others, in a one-on-one relationship, a small group, a class of children, or your family at home. Ask Him to reveal what specific formats and locations you can mentor in.
3. Ask God to continue giving you stories of answered prayer so you can share them with others as encouragement to keep hope alive.

TIME TO MENTOR

This section, at the end of each chapter, assumes you now are investing in a mentor group or individual mentee. Specific prompts can facilitate teaching your mentees. Also, you can reproduce the handouts at the end of the book to guide discussions or use as take-home assignments. Consider the following ideas as you begin to mentor.

1. Keep journaling your prayer experiences and answers in the back of this book.
2. Introduce yourself in the first session and describe your heart for prayer. Why did you start mentoring?

3. Invite group members to share about their personal prayer lives. Are they somewhat experienced or completely intimidated? Ask them to share joys, struggles, and fears.

4. Reassure your mentees you will learn along with them. Encourage them to take notes and write their stories of answered prayer. Explain that God could be preparing them to become mentors, too.

CHAPTER 2

You Pray Wrong!

I stood in front of a large class of adults at my church and wrote prayer requests on the whiteboard as people shared their concerns for others. I then invited group participation by covering the requests in a corporate time of prayer. After the flow of intercession ceased, I closed our time with a wrap-up prayer.

As I dismissed the group, a man strode up the center aisle toward me. It was one of those moments when you wonder if you are about to get a hug or a poke in the eye.

It certainly wasn't a hug.

"You pray wrong!" he exclaimed as he pointed his finger and gestured accusingly. I felt awkward, and glad most people had cleared out of the room.

He marched up to the whiteboard and grabbed a marker. "Here's how you pray," he said and scrawled these words: "Lord, I ask that You would _____."

"That's wrong!" he continued. "You need to pray more direct like this: 'Lord, do this _____.' People listen to you and respect you, and you are teaching them to pray without faith."

Too stunned to speak, I couldn't think clearly about a rebuttal or a theological perspective about prayer. Then he turned around and confidently walked out of the room, leaving me with swirling thoughts. The accusation, "You pray wrong," flooded my mind.

I served on the church staff, leading the adult ministries. I often stood in front of the congregation during worship services to lead prayer. *Was it true?* I thought. *And does everyone else think the same way about my prayer leadership?*

That incident paralyzed my prayer life. I stopped praying out loud, even in staff meetings. For days, I wrestled with accusing thoughts and the inability to be vulnerable in prayer.

The following week a close friend stopped by my office to visit me. She did not attend my church, so I worked up the courage to pose the question I dreaded to ask.

"Um, Gretchen, do I pray wrong?"

"Oh, for heaven's sake," she replied. "That's ridiculous."

Instantly, the lie's power over me broke. I realized I'd listened to Satan's accusations and allowed them to paralyze me.

It was a defining moment. I resolved not to let the enemy discourage me or someone else in prayer. If people hope to mature in prayer, they need encouragement to keep growing and stretching—and I am not the judge of their effectiveness!

LET'S ESTABLISH THIS

That experience turned into the basis of the first lesson I developed for my mentoring group. If mentees walk away with just one key principle in six months of mentoring, I want them to grasp this: *If you are praying at all, and your heart is for the Lord, you are praying right!*

Can we learn and grow in our prayer lives? Certainly. Can techniques and resources enhance our prayer? Yes, the ways to pray and approach the Lord seem endless. Are there times when we do not receive answers to our prayers because we pray with wrong motives (Jas. 4:3), or cherish unconfessed sin (Ps. 66:18)? Of course, at times we all struggle with the right words or heart attitude when we pray.

But God, a gracious and loving Father, delights to hear us pray. If you love the Lord and want to voice your heart to Him, He "bends down to listen." As the psalmist says, don't hesitate to "pray as long as [you] have breath" (Ps.116:2, NLT).

FINDING THE RIGHT WORDS

I confess that sometimes when I pray in a group, I grow conscious of my words. I focus more on how I say my prayer rather than allowing the Spirit to lead me. And sometimes I ramble, repeat myself, use annoying catch phrases, and just can't quite "land that plane."

In those times, I need to remember God doesn't answer my prayer because I impress Him with the fabulous way I worded it. He doesn't wait for me to present every possible option, so He can carefully consider and weigh each one, glean from my wise input, and then make His final decision. Sometimes I need to use fewer words and pray in simple faith, beyond my wisdom and understanding.

I served in the prayer ministry at a church several years ago with a wonderful team of intercessors. We prayed during the service in a conference room, and then moved to the front of the church's worship center to pray with people at the end of each service.

One Sunday a woman hesitantly approached our group and explained she felt embarrassed about her request. She would leave on a missions trip that week, and the weather forecast showed record heat, well over 100 degrees.

"I know this seems silly," she said, "but I really don't do well in the heat. I'm so stressed about it."

We gathered around her to pray. We offered great prayers about God sustaining her, giving her joy in whatever the circumstance, quelling her stress, and trusting God to care for her. We said heartfelt prayers. We said "right" prayers, rooted in Scripture.

Then the Holy Spirit impressed on me to pose a question.

"What temperature would you like it to be?" I asked.

She looked up, a bit surprised. "Well, 80s would be nice."

"Lord, I ask for 80s this week." That was it. For once I landed that plane quickly!

The following week she visited us again after the worship service, beaming with a huge smile.

"Guess what?" she said. "It was in the 80s and perfect!"

Sometimes we spend too much time searching for the right words—and miss the simplicity of God waiting for us to ask Him to display His love and power.

YOU ARE NOT ME, THANKFULLY!

Just so you know, I'm not an expert in prayer. (Just stating the obvious.) But I would call myself a "prayer practitioner." I try to learn about the many ways to pray, and then practice them. As a mentor, I favor different kinds of prayer based on my experience. I will most likely teach these principles to others because I enjoy incorporating them into my own prayer life. If you mentor someone, you will share different experiences than mine, along with selected ways you feel most comfortable while praying. When you pray, convey your unique self.

My mom prays with lists. She keeps in her Bible a calendar of people she prays for over the course of a month. Thankfully, her family appears on the daily list—often twice a day! She lists others she prays for on Mondays and other days of each week, and then people she intercedes for on the first of the month, the second of the month, and so forth. If you get on her prayer list, you don't get off until God miraculously transforms your life, or takes you home to heaven. She prays faithfully and tenaciously for others.

In contrast, I keep a much shorter list, with no guarantee you will stay on it forever. My mom's list remains rock solid and never-changing; mine is more fluid and in the moment. We practice prayer differently, and God answers us both. In fact, He answers many methods of prayer, even the ones I might not feel comfortable using.

Several years ago, I joined a group of people who loved a "listening" kind of prayer, centering around Scripture and periods of silence. This group met early in the morning (which admittedly turned into a struggle for me), and spent at least a half hour in silence while reflecting on Scripture or listening to the Spirit's voice. Then group members shared how the Lord's presence refreshed them during that time.

Often, I felt like the only group member who never fully grasped the morning's flow. I sometimes dozed, no matter how hard I tried to stay alert. Regardless of what I ate for breakfast, my stomach growled in the silence. I tried eating nothing, or loaded up on oatmeal, toast, and caffeine, but nothing made a difference. I felt like a perpetual distraction to the group.

Still, I gleaned insights from our sessions together. I appreciated the introspective approach, and at times, I still incorporate it in my prayer life. However, that type of prayer doesn't top my list for mentoring others. Instead, I draw from prayer approaches that most enhance my prayer life, and I eagerly share them.

God especially wired me to enjoy corporate prayer times, whether with one other person over the phone, or a small group gathered at my church. I love praying with other people. And I feel like my prayers soar with the most hope and expectancy when I'm praying for revival and spiritual awakening. God has planted that in my heart, and so it is one of the key ways I like to encourage others to pray.

God wired you with a specific design for prayer, too.

YOUR PRAYER PERSONALITY

Our personalities, temperaments, and prayer experiences figure into how we most comfortably intercede. God will undoubtedly stretch you in your prayer life, but you probably feel most called to pray in a certain style.

I call this a "prayer personality." When you listen to a variety of prayer approaches, you probably most identify with a few of them. I don't believe you need to dig too deeply into your temperament or take a personality test to figure out your prayer personality (although personality tests can be fascinating and helpful tools). But I do believe the key is to recognize you are not going to pray like everyone else—and then be okay with that!

When you look at some key biblical characters and how they prayed, varied personalities emerge. They probably didn't spend time studying how they prayed compared to others; they simply engaged their hearts with God in the moment. On the other hand, we can study and glean helpful observations from their prayer lifestyles.

I encourage you to pay attention to biblical people whose prayers resonate the most with you. Obviously, various circumstances call for different ways of praying, but you will most likely notice a style that fits your personality and comfort for expressing yourself in prayer.

LET'S EXPLORE

Read the following Scripture passages and write down everything you notice about each person's personality: how he or she prayed, and how it characterized his or her prayer personality. I included a few thoughts for each one, but you can find more. Discuss your findings with others.

1. **Mary.** Luke 1:46-55; 2:19: Trusting. Humbled to be chosen. Held things quietly in her heart. Faithful. Praiseful. Introspective. Confident.

2. **Anna.** Luke 2:36–38: Always fasted and prayed. Never gave up hope. Faithful every day. Persistent and expectantly waited. Allowed no distractions.

3. **Daniel.** Daniel 6:6–11; 10:1–14: Loyal. Faithful. Thankful. Fearless. Depended on God. Humble. Disciplined.

4. **Moses.** Exodus 32:30-32; 34:4-9: Pled and interceded on behalf of others. Worshiper.

5. **Elijah.** 1 Kings 18:30–39: Confident. Simple, bold prayer for the glory of God.

6. **Nehemiah.** Nehemiah 1:4–11: Acknowledged God's sovereignty. Confessed his sin and the sins of the nation. Patient; waited months for the answer. Held God accountable to His promises.

7. **Paul.** Ephesians 1:15–23; 3:14–21: Prayed for God's Kingdom. Blessed others. Drew on God's power. Grateful for God's gracious gifts.

8. **David.** Psalm 25, 86, 139: Expressed feelings: joy, despair, worship; all over the emotional map. Yet in whatever condition, with the Spirit's inspiration, the psalmist and king wrote down his rich prayer life.

Don't allow paralysis in your prayer life over fear that you might pray wrong. If your heart seeks the Lord, your prayer brings joy to Him—whatever you sound like!

THINK ABOUT IT

Consider the biblical people and their prayers again, and identify your own prayer personality.

1. Which biblical character's prayer personality fits most with your heart and experience? (Or perhaps choose more than one.) Describe that prayer personality. List the strengths of your prayer

life and celebrate the way God created you.

2. Which prayer personality intrigues you, but doesn't necessarily resemble you? Pray about how God might expand your prayer practices. List ways you want to grow in prayer.

PRAYER RESPONSE

How do you feel about your prayer personality? Talk to God about it, and how you can appreciate the way you naturally pray.

1. Thank God for the unique ways He gifted you. Celebrate your prayer personality. Invite God to grow your confidence in prayer.

2. If you hesitate to pray out loud in a group, ask God to transform you in the coming weeks. The next time you participate in a group, be the first to pray aloud, without hesitation. The more you jump in, the easier it will get.

TIME TO MENTOR

In your next meeting with your mentoring group, include these questions in the discussion.

1. Give your mentees insight into your prayer life. Share about your prayer personality. Has it changed over time? Or, perhaps you employ more than one based on different circumstances.

2. Describe what you observe about others in the way they pray (in your group, or just with you). Gently affirm group members' prayer personalities, reminding them God delights in their individual paths to Him.

CHAPTER *3*

How Big Is Your Vision?

Several years ago, a documentary about a Guatemalan community transformed by prayer captured my heart.[1] Guatemalans testified to the presence of Christ permeating the streets, along with an abundance of God's blessing and the "healing of the land." When I heard this story, something stirred in me. If it was true, I wanted to witness it firsthand.

My interest especially piqued because my family hosted an exchange student from Guatemala when I was in junior high school. Omar now works as a surgeon in Guatemala City and our family remains close to him. I knew if I wanted to visit this community in the mountains of Guatemala, Omar could help me get there.

I arranged for a trip with three other people: a ten-year-old boy named Nathanael, his mom, and a friend who spoke Spanish. (Confession: This was my moment of regret for not paying more attention during my four years of high school Spanish!)

We flew to Guatemala City, and then Omar drove us three hours through the mountains to Almolonga, a community with a population of around 15,000 people. He checked things out, made sure we felt settled and secure, and then left us with a cell phone as we set out to explore the town for the next three days. This was my dreamed-about opportunity to walk the streets, interact with the people, hear their stories, and discover for myself if the presence of Christ can truly transform an entire community.

According to the documentary, Almolonga's history is steeped in idol worship, abuse, crime, drunkenness, poverty, and over-crowded jails. The people drove out missionaries and persecuted the few believers in the community. Almolonga seemed a hopeless place until a pastor—under threats against his life—cried out to God in desperation. He mobilized his small congregation to join him in praying and fasting for God to change their community, with prayer times often lasting late into the night. They took seriously the God-honoring principle of 2 Chronicles 7:14:

> "If my people, who are called by my name, will humble themselves and pray and seek my face and turn from their wicked ways, then I will hear from heaven, and I will forgive their sin *and will heal their land*" (italics added).

As these believers prayed, God moved in miraculous ways. He changed the hearts of people, restored their faith, brought salvation to the lost, and even transformed the culture and fabric of the town.

WITH MY OWN EYES

Now, a few decades later, we walked the streets and observed how Jesus changed everything. My heart soared as we engaged with people and learned that almost everyone has a story about how God has miraculously touched him or her with healing—often physically, but always spiritually.

These Almolongans eagerly shared their stories with us. Many of them pointedly said we must take a message back to Minnesota: "It's not about a program. You must humble yourselves and pray. *You must humble yourselves and pray.* There is no other way!"

The evidences of transformation grew so numerous, I could hardly take it all in. If you visit Almolonga today, you will encounter these signs of transformation:

- A large banner hanging over the main street as you enter town declares, "Jesus is Lord of Almolonga!"
- Once 30 bars populated the city. Most of those bars closed, replaced by at least 30 churches.
- All the jails closed because officials don't need them anymore. Crime is practically non-existent. In fact, the police no longer carry guns, just whistles to direct traffic.
- Many business owners renamed their stores with Christian references, such as Hallelujah Bakery.
- Although statistics vary, some claim that at least 80–90 percent of the people are now followers of Jesus Christ. Others say it is less than that. Whether over 50 percent or nearly 100 percent does not seem relevant because I witnessed the joy of the Lord in almost everyone I met. People often stopped us on the street to interact and offer to pray for us. They eagerly told their stories of God at work in their lives. In all our interactions, we met just one woman who claimed she did not follow Jesus.

No question, this community is transformed. Our first day in town overwhelmed us. Nathanael summed it up perfectly when he exclaimed, "Wow, I really need to get out more!"

BUT THERE'S MORE!

We intentionally stayed through market day on Saturday because we wanted to see evidences of the healing of the land. Earlier, we heard about the abundant vegetables and flowers the land now produces.

We'd watched a video of beets, carrots, and cabbages grown in abundance and enormous in size. Even outsiders call Almolonga the Vegetable Basket of the Americas and the Miracle City.

That description did not disappoint. We watched the bustle of market day, immediately impressed by a dramatically different work ethic compared to other nearby communities. The people hustled and carried heavy loads of produce. Excitement and energy swirled around us. Even children participated in the market. We observed the unity of families and the respect and obedience of children who joyfully helped their parents.

We also marveled at the dramatic size of produce. Cabbages enlarged to the size of basketballs; carrots as long and wide as men's arms; beets the size of softballs, and radishes as large as a fist. We stared in awe, not just at the size, but the abundance. Piles and piles, bags after bags.

How did this happen? The people of Almolonga testified to the land's healing. They claimed their growing cycles supernaturally reduced so farmers now harvest three crops instead of one. They described a renewed and fertile soil. And they gave all glory to God.

I can't explain it, but I can testify to seeing it. It's truly a story of God healing the land in response to His people who humbled themselves and prayed.

MY OWN MIRACLE

During our visit, a farmer welcomed us into his fields. He gestured and offered us a gift. He pulled large carrots out of the ground and handed them to us, with dirt still clinging to them. His children, with shy smiles, wanted their pictures taken with us. We thanked them for sharing the blessing of their land.

When we got back to our hotel, we washed the carrots in the sink and tried to decide what to do with them. We knew we could not bring produce back into the United States, but we asked God to allow us to use the carrots as a testimony of His miraculous work.

My friends returned to the U.S. five days earlier than me, as I stayed to spend time with Omar and his family in Guatemala City. When my friends arrived at customs in Atlanta, they waited next in line for baggage inspection. Suddenly, the customs officials announced they closed the line and allowed everyone to walk through without inspection. Confused, Nathanael's mom asked an official, "Don't you want to see what we've claimed on our forms?"

"Mom," Nathanael whispered, "don't you remember? We prayed!"

They emailed me about the great news of carrying their carrots into the U.S. Thrilled, I still wanted to bring my carrot into America.

As I flew into Houston, I declared a vegetable on the customs form. As the plane landed, I prayed and worried about how to appeal my case to the customs officials.

Then the Lord spoke quietly to my heart. "Don't worry about it. Trust Me."

I got in the customs line and waited my turn. The official asked if I was bringing any produce into the U.S.

"Yes, I am," I declared. "I have a carrot."

"You have a carrot?" she asked with surprise.

"Yes, and it is right here in the top of this bag," I replied as I pointed to my carry-on.

She reached into my bag and pulled it out. She exclaimed, "Oh, my goodness. Is this from that place in Guatemala where people say God has blessed the land?"

She held it up and got the attention of everyone in customs, including other officials.

"Everyone," she said, "the reason this carrot is so big is because God has blessed the land!"

I've always thought it best not to draw attention when passing through customs, but I guess it's okay if God is drawing all the glory to Himself!

She turned back to me. "I'm so sorry. I can't let you bring it in."

"That's okay," I replied, disappointed. "I understand. I just wanted to try."

She continued to hold the carrot in her hands. "Just a minute," she said.

She called other customs officials into a huddle. They pulled binders off the shelf, looking through them and conferring with one another.

Then she returned to me, carefully inspected my carrot, and handed it to me. When I thanked her, she said, "You be sure to tell people how God has blessed the land."

So, by order of the United States government, I returned home to tell the story and show the evidence of God's miraculous answer to the cries of people who prayed according to 2 Chronicles 7:14!

I had another request of God. I prayed He would allow me to keep the carrot for a year, so I could show it to people and testify to His miraculous power to transform a community. My friends' carrots lasted only a couple of months before they withered and had to be thrown out. They expected that.

But I received my own little miracle. My carrot stayed in great shape for 18 months by simply keeping it in the refrigerator. It was above and beyond what I asked of God, simply because He chose to delight my heart!

WHAT IS YOUR VISION?

We can pray for lots of things: protection for family members, salvation of unsaved loved ones, healing of the sick, restoration of marriages, the next generation to stay true to the faith. I keep these concerns on my prayer list and pray for them faithfully. At the same time, I've wondered, *Is there something more?*

The Guatemalan trip awakened me to hope for much more. God longs to see His Church revived and His people as agents of transformation in their communities. He longs to awaken lost people to their need for Him, in answer to our prayers. That's why prayer for revival and spiritual awakening ignited a passion in my heart and focused my prayers. God imprinted this burden and calling on my prayer life.

But what does this mean in terms of how to pray?

First, let's look at some definitions so we can pray with common language:

- **Revival.** If something thirsts for revival, it once lived but eventually died, or fell dormant. It needs new life breathed into it. Applied to the Church, people once alive in Christ grow dull to the Holy Spirit's work. To revive His people, God sovereignly works among them, moving in a unique way. He empowers believers with a refreshing of His Spirit, so they live as designed, for His purposes. Repentance characterizes revival because it generates a new awareness of God's holiness, and how far the Church strays from her first love of Jesus. A new boldness and confidence fills Christians to share Jesus with unbelievers. Revival always results in evangelism.

- **Spiritual Awakening.** A spiritual awakening occurs when an unusually large number of unbelievers accept Jesus Christ as Savior. A Great Awakening is a move of God that sweeps large portions of a nation. Many Christian leaders believe in praying toward another Great Awakening, and most people today have never experienced this kind of move of God. When praying for our nation, we're asking for a spiritual awakening, which happens in response to a revival of God's people. This explains why many strongly emphasize praying for revival.

- **Transformation.** A community transforms when the Church revives. The Spirit empowers God's people, and a spiritual awakening draws lost people to Jesus. When a community, overcome with the presence and power of Christ, dramatically changes on all levels of society—crime, family, government, poverty, and more—people recognize this radical transformation. That's what I witnessed in Almolonga.

HAVE YOU HEARD OF THE HEBRIDES?

One of my favorite revival stories happened in the Hebrides Islands off the coast of Scotland during 1948–52.[2] It began with two home-bound elderly sisters, one blind and the other severely hampered by arthritis. The sisters grieved the decline of their church and the lack of spiritual interest among the young people. The sisters prayed faithfully, often late into the night. God implanted a vision for revival in their hearts, and they cried out with faith and hope.

Eventually, they called their pastor to accountability by asking him to gather the elders of the church to pray. As the leaders of the church joined in prayer, God moved in tangible and powerful ways. The elders and pastor repented before God and humbled themselves in desperation over the condition of their community. Reportedly, during one of the prayer meetings, the home where they prayed shook, much like in Acts 4:31.

The reviving presence of God descended upon their church, community, and surrounding villages throughout the Hebrides. Stories emerged of people falling under such strong conviction of the Holy Spirit, they fell to their knees in the streets, begging for forgiveness.

In another instance, several young people drank and partied at a dance hall, unaware of the prayer meeting at the church across town.

Without explanation, the DJ stopped the music, the young people abandoned their drinks, and most gravitated toward the church. When the partiers arrived, much to the surprise of the praying congregants, someone preached the gospel to the younger generation and many accepted Christ.

Before long, God combined these believers' powerful prayers with the authoritative preaching of Duncan Campbell, summoned by the sisters to serve as an evangelist throughout the area. Although some churches first resisted the gospel, reports claim eventually the presence of God touched every village. Churches revived and townspeople spiritually awakened to Jesus. Renewed people reported such a sense of joy, they sang in the stores, at the bus stops, and in other public places.

It all started with the faith and conviction of two sisters who humbly offered themselves and their prayers as catalysts for revival.

WHAT FUELS YOUR PRAYERS?

Historical accounts of revival, coupled with witnessing a truly transformed community, have fueled my prayers for several years. Knowing about these events, I can't help but pray with hope for my own community. "Why not here?" I often ask the Lord.

Many factors contribute to a move of revival in a church and a spiritual awakening in a community, but it begins with a handful of people committed to God's glory manifested in their streets. We can work hard to change the world through politics or education. We can faithfully declare truth in a spiritually hostile community. God calls us to these activities because we shine as the light of Christ in the darkness, even if we garner minimal success. But when the fires of revival ascend upon a church and people in the power of the Holy Spirit proclaim the gospel, well, there's nothing like that transformational vision!

I want my prayers infused with the belief that yes, *Jesus truly changes everything!* Revival, spiritual awakening, and transformation may look different in my city compared to Almolonga or the Hebrides. But I believe 2 Chronicles 7:14 is a time-honored prayer principle because it reveres our timeless and eternal God.

The formula is simple, but the calling is dramatic and selfless. God's people must humble themselves in prayer with their eyes fixed on the Lord, their hearts desperate for His presence, a willingness to repent and turn from sin, and a belief God is not only capable, but willing to heal our land.

When God calls His people to pray, I believe He intends to answer them.

THINK ABOUT IT

Using these questions, think more about how God transforms His people through humility, repentance, and prayer.

1. Research some of the past revivals and Great Awakenings. Make notes about examples of the ways a society or a nation can transform through prayer:

    • First Great Awakening:

    • Second Great Awakening:

    • Hebrides Revival:

    • Azusa Revival:

    • Other revivals or awakenings:

2. Envision your church changed through revival. What characterizes a revived church?

3. If God awakened the spiritually lost in your community, what evidences might you see? How could that impact your church and its relationship to the community?

4. What if God transformed your city? Imagine and list some of the societal changes.

5. What might a spiritual awakening in our nation look like? Again, envision hopeful changes in society.

PRAYER RESPONSE

What might be your response to learning about revival and a spiritual awakening?

1. Ask God to expand your vision for revival. Pray for specific repentance and changes.

2. Memorize and pray according to 2 Chronicles 7:14.

TIME TO MENTOR

With your group, review the three spiritually transforming definitions presented in this chapter. Apply them to your community.

1. Help your mentees understand the difference between revival, spiritual awakening, and transformation. Demonstrate ways to pray according to each principle.

2. Discuss 2 Chronicles 7:14 by listing God's requirements before the conditional promise of healing the land. Ask your group to envision what their community might look like if healed by God.

CHAPTER 4

Contending in Prayer

After my trip to Almolonga, I told my story, displayed my carrot, and encouraged Christians to pray with greater faith for a movement of God in their churches and communities. But this also raised questions within me. Why don't we experience more of God's presence and life-giving power in the United States? Where is our desperation for God? What would transformation look like in my community?

Revival 101 says any hope for revival begins with me. I took seriously the admonishments from my Guatemalan friends: the only path to revival is humility and prayer. So, I prayed in new and fresh ways. I practiced a lifestyle of repentance. My prayer life was invigorated. I invited others to pray with me. And I remembered a quote from a prayer leader friend, Steve Hawthorne, that increased my desperation: "In drastic days, pray great things."

We certainly live in drastic days in our nation, so my prayers and vision for revival increased with fervency. After my trip, I eagerly wanted a spectacular move of God.

And then it happened.

A PRAYER ASSIGNMENT

Well, I'm not exactly sure how it happened. Gradually, I guess. God tugged at my heart with the thought that He was preparing me for an unusual prayer assignment. I understood this as an "obedience thing." I sensed Him asking me to pick up and move to a new community for a specific prayer assignment.

Change is not my favorite thing. Once a piece of furniture finds its spot in my home, there's no moving it. It's just fine where it is. Forever. I usually look for a new car only when my old one is totaled (rarely my fault, of course). And I used my popcorn pan from college for at least 25 years before I finally threw it out. It's embarrassing.

Now I sensed God asked me to move from my comfortable, easy-to-manage townhome. I can't fully explain how I knew this. But I recognize when the Spirit moves within me. I think about it continuously, and pray with increased anticipation. Over several weeks, God confirmed I needed to move, which required a next step of obedience.

I contacted a friend in the real estate business. I cried when I met with her and said I needed to put my townhome on the market and look for something else. It was a bit more emotional than I anticipated. Obedience can feel like that. Fortunately, she is an intercessor-type, so I didn't need a lot of the I-think-God-told-me explanation. She naturally trusted with me that this was the right next step.

Of course, I outlined my criteria for everything I wanted in a new townhome. I was willing to move, but not willing to give up my favorite things!

We looked at townhomes matching my description, including everything on one level, no stairs. But I didn't feel peace about any of them. As I drove around the next few weeks, my attention kept diverting to three-level townhomes on top of a hill, overlooking the downtown of this new community. *No way,* I thought. They offered nothing I hoped to find, and looked a tad ugly.

To my surprise, the Spirit kept drawing me to that complex. I finally drove through it, praying for any insight from God. And, wouldn't you know, He led me to a certain townhome. Interestingly, it occupied the high point of the complex, with the best view over the city. I wondered if God's assignment meant living in this place, and praying for the city's transformation from this vantage point.

Of course, it wasn't for sale. *Of course.*

I pursued the only action a not-so-normal person would do. I repeatedly pulled into the driveway under the cover of night—asking God to give me the townhome!

THE IDIOT FACTOR

I stopped looking at other townhomes because I increasingly felt convinced God wanted me to live in this place. I kept up with my secret "prayer drive-bys." For months. It got uncomfortable with my friends.

"We thought you were moving," they said. "How is the townhome search coming along?"

Shoot. Another thing about obedience: sometimes God asks you to do seemingly foolish things.

"Um, I *am* moving," I replied. "But the townhome I'm supposed to buy isn't on the market yet." *Great,* I thought. *Thanks, God. If I'm wrong about this, You still get to be God, but I look like an idiot. Just great.*

After a few months of feeling foolish, and doubting I heard God correctly, on a whim I asked some friends if they wanted to see where I would live. (I mean, why not go for broke with the idiot factor?) We drove by the townhome, just for fun.

To my shock, a for-sale sign stood in front of it. I stopped breathing for a moment. I felt a rush of panic. Stunned, I could barely form words. *Oh, dear Lord! I'm not ready for this. But at least maybe I'm not an idiot after all!*

I contacted my agent, and she delivered bad news. The town-home owners had already signed a purchase agreement and were waiting on the final inspection. The townhome I prayed for—the home supposed to be mine—slipped away from me.

WILLING TO CONTEND

As you can imagine, I sputtered despairing words at God. My prayers filled with heartbroken and confused expressions. And that's when I heard Him speak to me. A clear thought overwhelmed me.

Are you willing to contend for it?

I knew the Lord spoke to me. I didn't know what "contend" meant, but I told Him I'd do whatever He showed me.

That began my journey for the next three days of fasting, praying, crying out to God, and inviting others to join me in prayer. I also arranged a home showing so I could go into the townhome, kneel on the floor, and ask Him to give it to me. I spent my evenings on the floor in my own home, reading and praying Scripture and pleading with God for His intervention. I prayed with faith that God intended this townhome for me. I felt I contended with dark spiritual forces for the fulfillment of His promise to me.

After three days of prayer and fasting and contending in every way I could think of, the Lord spoke to me again, much like He did the first time about contending.

It's over. Stop contending and start worshiping Me with praise and thanksgiving.

Really, Lord? Was that Your voice I just heard?

The thought came to me again, even stronger this time. So, I asked God to confirm it in Scripture. I did what never works for me at any other times—and I don't recommend it as reliable. I blindly opened my Bible to an unknown spot and randomly pointed to a verse. My finger landed on Exodus 33:17 (TLB), when God spoke to

Moses: "I will do what you have asked, for you have found favor with me, and you are my friend."

I closed my Bible with a peace and confidence. I also stopped contending. I praised and thanked the Lord for what He had done.

Within just an hour, my agent called me with surprise in her voice. "We might have a very small shot at getting the townhome."

I replied, "I know. At 2:20 this afternoon the Lord told me to stop contending and start worshiping Him with praise and thanksgiving." (Again, I can't emphasize enough how glad I am my agent is an intercessor who gets the weird stuff!)

To our amazement, the buyer unknowingly defaulted on his purchase agreement by refusing to take the home "as is" after the inspection revealed a small issue: a loud garbage disposal. (No kidding—that was the main problem with the home, and the buyer refused to budge.) Because I made a full-price offer with no contingencies, the townhome was mine.

PERSISTENCE VS. CONTENDING

God taught me a crash course on what it means to contend in prayer. I learned that *contending is not the same as persisting*. We understand persistence in prayer, as demonstrated by the parable of the persistent widow (Luke 18:1–8). Jesus used this parable to teach the disciples how to pray without giving up. In this story, a widow returned to a judge again and again with her pleas for justice, until he finally relented and granted her desire because "she keeps bothering me" (vs. 5). In other words, her persistence drove the judge crazy and he dealt justice to keep her out of his courtroom.

It seems like an odd story for Jesus to tell in relationship to the disciples always praying. But He used it to encourage them: "And will not God bring about justice for his chosen ones, who cry out to him day and night? Will he keep putting them off?" (vs. 7).

In other words, *pray like a crazy person*. Don't give up. Don't stop asking God for that request near and dear to your heart. Jesus gives you permission to persist, which means to continue "especially past a usual, expected, or normal time."[3]

You can probably think of ways you've persisted in prayer. A loved one who strayed from the Lord. Family members hardened to the gospel. A difficult health situation. I downloaded an app on my phone that highlights different people at designated and random times during the day. It helps me to persistently pray for them. As I mentioned previously, my mom schedules who she prays for every day, those she prays for on a certain day of the week, and those she prays for monthly. She prays as systematically and persistently as anyone I know. You can develop your own ways of persistently praying for those you love.

On the other hand, contending in prayer demands even more. This kind of prayer rises in you with an intensity and fervency I sometimes refer to as "mama-bear praying." You probably know the kind. It's a Spirit-led, emotion-infused battle when you feel like you are taking on forces of evil, desperate for a breakthrough: "Not my child. Not my family. Not my nation!"

It is a more strategic, urgent, and desperate kind of praying. It's also not a sustainable way to pray over a long period of time because it becomes all-consuming, often coupled with fasting, sleepless nights, and agony of the soul. That's what makes contending different from persisting. For a moment or a season, you fight with all the resources of heaven on behalf of someone or something.

A COSMIC BATTLE

In Jude 3, believers were urged to contend for the faith because ungodly people and teaching had slipped into the church: "Dear friends, although I was very eager to write to you about the salvation we share, I felt compelled to write and urge you to contend for the faith that was once for all entrusted to God's holy people" (vs. 3).

Contending in this context refers to an intense effort like a wrestling match. My dad's high school wrestling career ended when a husky farm boy made the team. In the boy's first practice, he picked up my dad (who was quite a bit smaller) and forcefully threw him to the mat, breaking his collar bone. Not the true spirit of competitive wrestling.

I used to get on the floor and wrestle with my young nephews. For a season it was a harmless and fun interaction. But I remember when my nephew Brent asked me if I wanted to wrestle, and then told me to take off my glasses. I knew right then our wrestling days were over!

True wrestling is a picture of an ongoing struggle to maintain control or victory over an opponent. Neither participant is willing to give up until one is clearly pinned or defeated. Jacob wrestled all night with the Lord and did not give up until he was assured of God's blessing (Gen. 32:22–32).

When I contended in prayer for my townhome, I related to this definition of the word: "To strive in opposition or against difficulties; struggle: armies contending for control of territory."[4] That sums up how I felt—I was wrestling with spiritual powers in a battle for land and a desperate community. For whatever reason, this townhome occupied strategic territory, and for reasons known only to God, He assigned me to pray over the city from that crucial vantage point.

Contending engages in a cosmic battle for the advancement of God's Kingdom in people's lives. The prophet Daniel engaged in a cosmic battle. In Daniel 10, the prophet humbled himself, fasted, and prayed for 21 days. But until the angel Gabriel appeared to Daniel, he knew nothing about the heavenly battle raging around him.

When Gabriel finally greeted Daniel with a message from the Lord, the faithful pray-er learned the prince of Persia (a demonic entity) held Gabriel in check until the archangel Michael joined the battle for a breakthrough. Gabriel gave Daniel a glimpse of this cosmic battle (10:12–14):

> "Do not be afraid, Daniel. Since the first day that you set your mind to gain understanding and to humble yourself before your God, your words were heard, and I have come in response to them. But the prince of the Persian kingdom resisted me twenty-one days. Then Michael, one of the chief princes, came to help me, because I was detained there with the king of Persia. Now I have come to explain to you what will happen to your people in the future, for the vision concerns a time yet to come."

What? Does this really happen around us? Yes. If there was a war waging in Daniel's day, it certainly hasn't stopped in our day!

All Daniel did to put the battle into motion was pray. And pull out all the stops of fasting, humility, and continuous intercession. It was a 21-day season of contending that caused a shift in the heavenly realms.

In the same way, you may not know what goes on in the spiritual realm. But the Spirit moves you to fast, pray, plead, and intercede with everything you've got! That's contending in prayer.

STAYING HOPEFUL

You might think, *That's not me. My prayers could never have that kind of influence in the heavenly realms.*

Don't forget Daniel. I'm sure he didn't imagine an other-worldly, angelic struggle while he prayed. In fact, when Gabriel finally appeared to him, Daniel weakened, his face turned deathly pale, and he felt completely helpless. The passage says God put him into a deep sleep until the angel touched him (10:7–11). I think that means Daniel passed out. Cold. When the prophet recovered, he trembled on his hands and knees.

Imagine for a moment humbling yourself, fasting, praying, and pulling out all the stops you can think of as you intercede. Perhaps a cosmic battle will unfold in answer to your prayers.

It's not easy. At times, I get discouraged in my prayer life. I look around and see things getting worse rather than better. Loved ones sink deeper into sin. Our nation continues to tear itself apart with hatred, violence, and division. But I don't lose hope.

I look back to my previous experiences to gain faith for the future. I've witnessed what God can do in answer to contending prayer. I've walked the streets of a transformed community. I've lived in a townhome He prepared especially for me. I've read the stories of past revivals and spiritual awakenings in our nation. So even when I get tired and need refreshing in my prayer, I still hang on to hope.

That's because my hope doesn't rest in the effectiveness of my prayers, but instead in my God who always wins the cosmic battles. If I can engage in that battle by stepping into contending prayer, I want to intercede for the honor and glory of the name of Jesus!

MORE ABOUT THE TOWNHOME

Remember the loud garbage disposal? To my surprise, the sellers decided to replace it for me—I guess just because they could (or because God compelled them). I didn't ask. They offered.

When I attended the closing, I shared with the sellers that I prayed for their townhome. Late at night. In their driveway.

"That's so weird," said the wife. (Sigh. I know.) They looked shocked, and then remarked they never intended to move. The wife explained she woke up one morning with the urgent need to sell. Her husband resisted, not wanting to move. They'd just finished remodeling the townhome exactly as they wanted it. So why should they move?

But the wife insisted. "We *have* to move," she declared. They put the townhome on the market and bought the first home they walked through.

The husband looked at me. "I never wanted to move."

"I'm so sorry," I answered. Poor guy.

When we walked out of the closing, the husband pulled me aside. He took out his wallet and handed me a $10 bill. "I'm sorry," he confessed. "I broke the shade upstairs." I guess he figured since ultimately God managed this transaction—and apparently, I had a connection to God—he needed to make that right!

STAYING FAITHFUL IN PRAYER

I lived on that hill for eight years, contending in prayer for my community. I asked the Lord to help me offer great prayers in drastic times, prayers that God's glory would reign in my community. Others joined me in those prayers.

Then one summer God placed in my heart a desire to prayer-walk this community of 20,000 people. I got a map of the city and highlighted streets with a marker as I walked and prayed. It took four months, but I covered every street and prayed for each home. (Granted, sometimes I prayed I could just find my car again!)

When I finished covering the city in prayer, God prompted me to move again. I'd completed my assignment. I'd obeyed everything He asked of me, even though I'd not yet seen the answers. Sometimes God withholds immediate results from His people, as described in Hebrews 11:13: "All these people were still living by faith when they died. They did not receive the things promised; they only saw them and welcomed them from a distance, admitting that they were foreigners and strangers on earth."

I knew I could be content with God's timing and wisdom. I anticipated a new season in my life. I put my home on the market and moved to another community, where my church is now just around the corner. A new place with new adventures.

In God's economy, my only concern is obedience. For me, that means persistence in prayer always, and contending when the Spirit moves me to engage in a cosmic battle.

If your heart stays sensitive to God's voice, there will always be a next adventure. His Kingdom is not static, and His purposes always advance.

THINK ABOUT IT

Have you contended in prayer? Not everyone understands how to contend, so don't feel bad if it's not part of your prayer life yet. These questions focus on distinguishing between contending and persisting in prayer:

1. List some situations when you sensed God invited you to contend in prayer. Perhaps you contended for a family member, a difficult situation, or the condition of our nation. How did you contend? What did God lead you to pray?
2. Compare contending with how you've persisted in prayer. What differences did you experience?
3. Think of a time you prayed or did something out of obedience to God, and perhaps risked the "idiot factor." How did God spiritually grow you in that experience?

PRAYER RESPONSE

Anyone can contend in prayer. It's not just for a select few. God will guide you when it's time to pray fervently for a person or circumstance.

1. Ask the Lord for sensitivity to the Spirit to know when to contend for a certain place, people, or situation. When you discern it's time, pull out all the stops, pray with faith, and rest in God to fight a cosmic battle in answer to your prayers.

2. Also ask God to tell you when to stop contending. How will you know this?

TIME TO MENTOR

Your mentees might struggle with the difference between contending and persisting in prayer. Carefully listen to their responses and assist their understanding.

1. Explain the difference between contending and persisting in prayer to your mentees. Then give examples of when you employed the two different prayer strategies. If appropriate, ask for examples from them, too.

2. Read the Daniel 10 passage together in your group. Dig deeper into the ways Daniel prayed, and the amazing results of his contending in prayer.

CHAPTER 5

The Power of Praying Scripture

My dad confessed faith in Jesus as a high school student during a Billy Graham Youth for Christ meeting in Austin, Minnesota.

Well, not exactly.

His friend decided to go forward to the stage at the invitation to accept Christ, but she didn't want to walk alone. So, my dad accompanied her to the front, where they met a counselor trained to help people take the next steps to follow Jesus. After talking and praying with the friend, the counselor turned to my dad.

"How about you? Are you here to accept Christ, also?" the counselor asked.

"No, I'm fine," replied my dad.

Thankfully, Dad accepted a small booklet—the Gospel of John—and took it home with him.

That night, the Holy Spirit began His work. Dad read through the entirety of John in one sitting and the Word convicted him of hypocrisy. He knelt by the side of his bed and surrendered his life to Jesus.

If Scripture powerfully changed my dad's life in an instant—and in turn, generations after him—it also wields the power to transform anyone's prayer life.

MY JOURNEY THROUGH SCRIPTURE

During those months when I prayed and asked God to give me the townhome, the Spirit convicted me of a lack of spiritual preparation for the approaching prayer assignment. I didn't fully understand what lay ahead, but I knew I needed to act.

I did the most strategic thing I knew to do. I unplugged my television for a season and started praying through the Bible. I'd never attempted this before, but I began in Genesis 1 because, *why not?* I read passages of Scripture, paused, asked the Spirit to lead me, prayed what came to mind, made notes in the margins, and turned many verses into prayers.

I'm not going to lie. Leviticus was hard. I didn't write much in the margins throughout that book.

Yet, as I prayed through the Bible, God profoundly changed my heart. I fell even more in love with Jesus as He revealed Himself to me through His Word.

As I prayed through the Old Testament, I embraced repentance, obedience, holiness, and fear of the Lord as characteristics to mark my life as a believer. I prayed for the faith demonstrated by early God followers. I read about spiritual battles the biblical patriarchs faced, and how they looked to God as their deliverer. I prayed through the common theme of disaster striking when someone takes his or her eyes off the Lord. Enemies turn into victors, people rebel, and ungodly strongholds rise up. It's ugly. But God redeems.

When I prayed through the New Testament, my longing for the manifest presence of Jesus Christ through revival consumed my prayers. I invited Jesus to warm my heart with greater compassion toward the lost and hurting. I prayed for the courage and boldness demonstrated by early followers of Christ when enemies threatened and harassed them because of the gospel. I asked God to bless me with even a fraction of the apostle Paul's prayer life, as demonstrated in his epistles.

After three years—yes, it took three years—I finally prayed the ultimate invitation at the end of Revelation: "Come, Lord Jesus" (Rev. 22:20).

I now cherish a Bible full of notes, highlights, and dates because praying Scripture taught me to hear God's voice in prayer. He speaks through His Word. This anonymous quote sums it up well: "One should never read the Bible without praying, and never pray without reading the Bible." Praying Scripture is one of the best ways to hear God's voice.

I believe this general principle: If your prayer life rarely stems from your time in the Word, most of your prayers probably focus on asking God for things: "Help me; I need You to fix this situation; so and so needs to stop living a disastrous life; please provide the finances I need this month." These represent appropriate prayers, but adding the Scripture component assures you align with God's purposes, His plans, His desires, and the advancement of His Kingdom.

If you don't get anything else from this chapter, at least clutch your Bible when you pray. The Holy Spirit will take over from there.

LEARNING FROM THE BEST

For a season, God placed me under the mentorship of Evelyn Christenson, an international prayer leader who wrote the classic, *What Happens When Women Pray,* and served as a founding member of America's National Prayer Committee. For the last few years of Evelyn's life, I met monthly with this prayer warrior and her ministry board at an assisted-living complex. For the most part, I just listened to Evelyn pray and share stories from her lifetime of ministry.

At the end of Evelyn's life, her family summoned board members to say goodbye. I'd always hoped she would pray over me, but never felt comfortable asking her. That seemed a bit self-serving. Instead, in my final moment with Evelyn, I knelt beside her and mentioned my gratitude for how she'd blessed me with her example. I said I loved her, and then stood up to leave. A line of people stood behind me, so I didn't want to overextend my time.

I don't know how Evelyn mustered the strength, but she grabbed me by the neck, put me in a headlock, pulled me close, and said a beautiful prayer over me. It was perfect. Then she loosened her grip, patted my shoulder, and said, "There. You're ready to go."

Evelyn's last words to me exceeded my heart's desire.

I learned from Evelyn that praying according to God's Word equates to praying in the Spirit. Who inspired the writing of Scripture? The Holy Spirit. Therefore, praying back the truths of Scripture assures praying according to God's Kingdom purposes. You can't go wrong using the words inspired by the triune God. The more you know Scripture and incorporate it into prayers, the more you will pray with power and authority.

At Evelyn's memorial service, the family displayed her Bible along with photos and memories. It was stunning to see every page of her Bible highlighted with multiple colors and filled with her personal prayers. Her Bible was part of her legacy she left with her family.

As I've grown in my appreciation for Scripture and its connection to powerful prayer, I've discovered several additional reasons to incorporate God's Word into my prayers. Maybe you will benefit from these highlights, modeled by early believers:

1. Scripture helps me pray when I'm not sure what to say. You've had those moments when your voice seems inadequate. Perhaps you feel overwhelmed by tragedy or struggles. You might feel confused by a seemingly hopeless situation. Or, you simply can't relate to someone else's experience. You have no idea how to pray. I often feel I can't totally relate when I pray for the persecuted Church, for those believers under the duress of hatred, prison, torture, and death.

Of what possible use are my inadequate prayers?

When I ask this question, I need to remember every prayer counts, even when I don't know what to say.

Perhaps the disciples and early believers didn't know how to pray when authorities released Peter and John from prison, but threatened them not to speak about Jesus again (Acts 4:18). But these believers hearkened back to God's past faithfulness, and relied on Scripture to call upon God in their time of need.

As soon as Peter and John returned to their fellow believers and reported the threats of the chief priests and elders, the people lifted their voices in scriptural prayers. They quoted from Exodus 20:11 and Psalm 2:1–2:

> When they heard this, they raised their voices together in prayer to God. "Sovereign Lord," they said, "you made the heavens and the earth and the sea, and everything in them. You spoke by the Holy Spirit through the mouth of your servant, our father David:
> 'Why do the nations rage
>   and the peoples plot in vain?
> The kings of the earth rise up
> and the rulers band together
> against the Lord
> and against his anointed one.'

Indeed, Herod and Pontius Pilate met together with the Gentiles and the people of Israel in this city to conspire against your holy servant Jesus, whom you anointed. They did what your power and will had decided beforehand should happen" (Acts 4:24–28).

Then the believers formed their request, based on a foundation of Scripture:

"Now, Lord, consider their threats and enable your servants to speak your word with great boldness. Stretch out your hand to heal and perform signs and wonders through the name of your holy servant Jesus." After they prayed, the place where they were meeting was shaken. And they were all filled with the Holy Spirit and spoke the word of God boldly (vss. 29–31).

At their greatest moment of need, they prayed Scripture! This was a deciding moment for them. Will the gospel go forth by their witness, or will they cower in fear? They turned to Scripture to form their bold prayer to keep moving forward in power.

Think about this reality check. We might experience more persecution in the days to come. It almost seems inevitable because we already witness an increased hostility in the media and our culture. So now is the time to learn to pray in power and confidence through Scripture.

2. Scripture enriches the content of my prayers. At a prayer gathering with pastors and ministry leaders, a facilitator instructed us to spend time just praying Scripture. Several people prayed aloud in our group of about 50 people. I noticed everyone opened to a favorite passage of Scripture, read it aloud word for word, and then added an amen at the end. They prayed God's Word, so of course, each prayer sounded beautiful.

Then an elderly man stood up and prayed a Scripture passage by incorporating his own words. He prayed a scriptural phrase, added his heartfelt imploring to God, added more Scripture, and pleaded with the Lord again from his own emotion and desire. The man seamlessly intertwined God's Word and his words. It flowed out of him, a beautiful expression I'd never heard before.

Okay, now *that* was praying Scripture!

You might aspire to praying Scripture like this man, but right now it seems beyond your ability. Don't panic. Don't make it complicated. It's not about memorizing vast amounts of Scripture, although I love praying with people with that amazing capacity. It's precious to hear them quote Scripture in their prayers.

For most of us, though, we will pray around concepts. Or we will pray with a Scripture passage open in our laps, adding our personal touches.

Let's use Paul's prayer in Ephesians 1:15–23 as an example:

For this reason, ever since I heard about your faith in the Lord Jesus and your love for all God's people, I have not stopped giving thanks for you, remembering you in my prayers. I keep asking that the God of our Lord Jesus Christ, the glorious Father, may give you the Spirit of wisdom and revelation, so that you may know him better. I pray that the eyes of your heart may be enlightened in order that you may know the hope to which he has called you, the riches of his glorious inheritance in his holy people, and his incomparably great power for us who believe. That power is the same as the mighty strength he exerted when he raised

Christ from the dead and seated him at his right hand in the heavenly realms, far above all rule and authority, power and dominion, and every name that is invoked, not only in the present age but also in the one to come. And God placed all things under his feet and appointed him to be head over everything for the church, which is his body, the fullness of him who fills everything in every way.

Right now, sit with this passage. Read it several times. Invite the Holy Spirit to open your eyes and heart to how you can pray these verses for yourself and others. Jot notes about some basic concepts Paul conveys in this passage.

Now turn your notes into a prayer, incorporating the concepts and principles Paul used. Pray for yourself. Insert personal pronouns. Pray for someone else by inserting that person's name. Form your prayers with a Spirit-led infusion of the same hope Paul displayed.

Did you enrich your prayer's content? You might not naturally think to pray with Paul's terms, so let the Spirit and the Word help you.

3. Scripture focuses me on praying beyond my "fix-it" pleas to Kingdom prayers. I first heard the term "fix-it" prayer from my colleague Jon Graf, publisher of *PRAY* magazine. I can't think of a better way to label it, so I'll give him credit, and then use it.

Fix-it prayers long for God to change a circumstance, heal a situation, or intervene in a place of hopelessness. I pray fix-it prayers all the time. They truly express the desires of my heart. But I also want to pray beyond my needs, recognizing God's purpose in everything happening to me and others. I want to offer up Kingdom prayers.

One of my favorite examples of a Kingdom prayer is Jesus praying for Simon Peter. As Jesus celebrated Passover with His disciples in the Last Supper together, He spoke about His impending death.

The disciples didn't grasp what Jesus said, and instead, bickered about who was the greatest among them. They remained clueless.

That's when Jesus shared something profound with Peter. He said: "Simon, Simon, Satan has asked to sift all of you as wheat. But I have prayed for you, Simon, that your faith may not fail. And when you have turned back, strengthen your brothers" (Lk. 22:31–32).

Jesus knew what lay ahead for Peter. However, He didn't pray for God to fix it so that Peter could escape pain. Instead, Jesus prayed Peter would not lose his faith after he denied the Lord in the most heartbreaking moment of his life. At some point, before this final time together, Jesus prayed for Peter. He foresaw Peter's role in eventually strengthening and encouraging believers to stay strong during opposition. Jesus prayed beyond Peter's pain and into God's plans for him.

Jesus set a good example for us. Instead of praying for others to live free of pain and struggle—which we're tempted to ask for our loved ones—use Scripture to pray in advance for God to turn heartache and struggle into Christ-like transformation and Kingdom advancement.

I think of a Kingdom prayer as a "so that" prayer. When you pray for someone or something, add the words "so that" and then fill in the blank. Why are you praying this request, beyond the obvious, immediate need? Ask God for something grand and wonderful in people's lives so that they honor and glorify God and advance His Kingdom.

Paul added a so-that conclusion to some of his prayers: "May the God who gives endurance and encouragement give you the same attitude of mind toward each other that Christ Jesus had, *so that* with one mind and one voice you may glorify the God and Father of our Lord Jesus Christ (Rom. 15:5–6, italics added).

How does your life measure up with fix-it prayers vs. Kingdom prayers? Try adding a "so that" to your prayers and watch God expand your Kingdom perspective.

4. Scripture offers me a language of praise. I confess I'm not great at praise. I enjoy praying with people who are wonderfully expressive in their prayers. It feels like their worship ushers me into the throne room of God.

On the other hand, I often stumble around for praise language, and my prayers can sound like this: "God, You are awesome and powerful, Creator of the universe, in charge of everything, and, um, really big. And, um, I'm not sure what else to say, but You are just, like, great."

It leaves a bit to be desired. I'm probably getting better at praise, but most of the time I don't feel my words adequately express my heart. For sure, I don't feel I give God the glory He deserves.

That's when I use my "cheat sheet." It's called *The Psalms*.

If you want to increase your praise vocabulary, use psalms in your prayers. David wrote many of them. God endowed David with gifted and artistic language—and He inspired David to write down his praise. When you use psalms as the basis for your worship and praise, your heart can soar.

As an exercise, open your Bible to Psalm 98 or 145. Get a cup of coffee, settle in, read through the psalm several times, and jot notes. Then write your own prayer of praise. Pray it back to the Lord and enjoy enhanced language that more closely matches your heart and love for God.

5. Scripture frames how I pray for people on my prayer list. The apostle Paul rarely prayed for physical needs. If I'd lived through Paul's circumstances, I'd ask never to be beaten, imprisoned, or shipwrecked again. And I would pray the same for my friends.

But Paul was more concerned about spiritual health than physical needs. While I want to continue praying for those personal needs, I also want to pray beyond that. Unfortunately, I can easily find myself praying for the same things over and over again—and then tacking on, "and God bless them." That really doesn't express the desire of my heart for their spiritual needs. Praying Scripture allows me to be more specific in *how* I desire God to bless them with all the riches of heaven.

One of my "go-to" passages in praying for spiritual growth is Colossians 1:9–12:

> For this reason, since the day we heard about you, we have not stopped praying for you. We continually ask God to fill you with the knowledge of his will through all the wisdom and understanding that the Spirit gives, so that you may live a life worthy of the Lord and please him in every way: bearing fruit in every good work, growing in the knowledge of God, being strengthened with all power according to his glorious might so that you may have great endurance and patience, and giving joyful thanks to the Father, who has qualified you to share in the inheritance of his holy people in the kingdom of light.

If you want to add to the "God bless" prayer that perhaps you typically pray, try using this Scripture passage for those special people who are always on your heart.

6. Scripture helps me repent more. Sometimes I just need a good cleansing. There's probably no better passage I pray than Psalm 51. David thoroughly repented, and this can be the basis for your confession and repentance, too. Read these verses as a sample:

> Have mercy on me, O God,
>   according to your unfailing love;
>   according to your great compassion
>   blot out my transgressions.
> Wash away all my iniquity

and cleanse me from my sin.
For I know my transgressions,
  and my sin is always before me.
Against you, you only, have I sinned
  and done what is evil in your sight;
so you are right in your verdict
  and justified when you judge.
Surely I was sinful at birth,
  sinful from the time my mother conceived me.
Yet you desired faithfulness even in the womb;
  you taught me wisdom in that secret place.
Cleanse me with hyssop, and I will be clean;
  wash me, and I will be whiter than snow.
Let me hear joy and gladness;
  let the bones you have crushed rejoice.
Hide your face from my sins
  and blot out all my iniquity.
Create in me a pure heart, O God,
  and renew a steadfast spirit within me (vss. 1-10).

We need to develop a lifestyle of humility and repentance, and this passage will help frame that for you. It will make you aware of spiritual barriers, and more:

- Your sin and heart attitude.
- How far you've departed from God.
- How little you truly trust His character.
- Your fears and doubt.
- How much pride you harbor.

And the list goes on. When you start repenting, God tends to bring things up! Mark this psalm in your Bible and tuck it away as a reminder to continually cleanse your heart. Greater repentance yields greater prayer.

THAT'S JUST CRAZY!

A few years ago, I participated in a Bible study on the life of Moses. As I worked through the Book of Exodus, chapter by chapter, I found an earlier note I wrote in the margin of my Bible near Exodus 33:1–5 (NLT):

> Then the Lord said to Moses, "Look, I have specifically chosen Bezalel son of Uri, grandson of Hur, of the tribe of Judah. I have filled him with the Spirit of God, giving him great wisdom, ability, and expertise in all kinds of crafts. He is a master craftsman, expert in working with gold, silver, and bronze. He is skilled in engraving and mounting gemstones and in carving wood. He is a master at every craft!"

I'd written my friend Evan's name next to the passage, with a date from a few years earlier. Obviously, I prayed these verses for Evan, but I didn't remember why. I emailed him and asked what happened in his life at that time, and why God prompted me to pray these specific verses for him.

"That's just crazy!" he emailed back. Evan visited Bolivia at that time, recording an album for a church. As a sound engineer, he used his skills to produce a professional recording. In pulling the album together, Evan ended up having to play and record a variety of instruments that he was not necessarily skilled in playing. For that moment, he needed to be a "master at every craft."

I had no idea about this musical need when I prayed for Evan. But the Lord knew. Using my Bible as a basis for prayer, beyond my understanding, God directed me to mark and pray those specific words for my friend.

God's Word is inspired, powerful, and the perfect prayer guide for any situation. The more you incorporate Scripture into your prayers, the greater your Kingdom reach!

THINK ABOUT IT

Practice praying Scripture with well-known and favorite passages. Notice how God's Word enriches your prayers.

1. You've probably memorized—or at least read many times—the Lord's Prayer from Matthew 6:9–13:

> "This, then, is how you should pray:
> 'Our Father in heaven,
> hallowed be your name,
> your kingdom come,
> your will be done,
>   on earth as it is in heaven.
> Give us today our daily bread.
> And forgive us our debts,
>   as we also have forgiven our debtors.
> And lead us not into temptation,
>   but deliver us from the evil one.'"

Begin using this passage for praying Scripture at multiple times during the day. Instead of just quoting it, incorporate your own words. Personalize it while washing dishes, sorting your office desk, or driving to yet another baseball practice. For instance, pray something like this:

"I come to You as my Father who reigns and rules in heaven and over all things. I love You and praise You with all my heart. I long for Your Kingdom to come in such a way, it changes everything around me and people turn their hearts toward You. I may not always be great at discerning Your will in my life, but I do desire that You transform me by Your will.

"And what are some of the ways that I long to see Your will done? Well, I pray that all my family members embrace You, Jesus, as both Savior and Lord. I pray my life is characterized by radical obedience to You. Show me each day how You want me to respond to others You place in my path.

"I want to say out loud to You that I trust You for my daily provision. I believe You will provide everything my family needs. I am grateful for how You even provide the food I set before my family on the dinner table tonight.

"And You know I struggle with forgiveness in some instances. As You bring people to mind right now, I will take the faith step of praying for my heart to radically reset with forgiveness. Help me to keep a short list of offenses. Okay, a non-existent list!

"And Lord, every day I need Your help to overcome temptation and to keep from slipping into sin. You know my habitual sins, and I pray for once-and-for-all deliverance from them. [List them here.] I pray for healing and freedom.

"Everything I am and have is rooted in my love and praise for You. My future is secure in You, and I pray that I will live with confidence in Your Kingdom reigning forever! Amen."

You get the idea. Let the Lord's Prayer guide your ongoing dialogue with God. Use this as an example to show others how to pray Scripture, based on how it formed your prayer language.

2. Now pick a book of the Bible and pray through it. Then pray through another book, chapter by chapter. Ask the Lord if He wants you to pray through the entire Bible—or a specific book or section—regardless of how long it takes.

PRAYER RESPONSE

Ask God to give you a passion for His Word—to read it, allow the Spirit to speak to you through it, and incorporate it into your prayer life. Choose passages that speak to you, and pray them back to God.

TIME TO MENTOR

Encourage your group to pray with Scripture, even with a few verses. Share your experiences, and talk about moving beyond fix-it prayers toward Kingdom prayers.

1. Look through your Bible and note any highlighted verses or notes in the margins. Record the reasons you prayed those specific Scripture passages. Share examples with your mentor group.
2. Discuss with your group fix-it prayers vs. Kingdom prayers. Give examples of the difference. Practice adding "so that" to your requests, turning them into Kingdom prayers. Encourage your group to practice praying beyond fix-it prayers.
3. Read the Lord's Prayer aloud with your group, taking turns to personalize it. Affirm efforts to frame their prayers with Scripture.

CHAPTER 6

Jesus, the Greatest Intercessor

I confess. I've thought about it more than once: *Why in the world did the three disciples fall asleep while Jesus prayed in the Garden of Gethsemane? Really? How could they not stay awake for even an hour during Jesus' moment of great need?*

How hard can it be?

Early one morning, I got my answer. I crawled into bed the night before with a heavy burden on my heart. At about 2:00 a.m., I still could not sleep. I got out of bed, knelt on the floor in my bedroom with my face in the carpet, and cried out to God to intervene in a difficult situation. I prayed and stormed the gates of heaven with passion and loud cries.

And then I woke up about 20 minutes later.

I could not feel my legs. Both were numb and completely useless. Still in a kneeling position, I reached back behind me, picked up a leg, and dropped it with a dead thud. The other leg responded with the same thud. I panicked. *Oh, dear. Is it possible to paralyze myself?*

I rolled over on my side and dragged myself toward the bed. That's when my "dead" legs started to wake up. You know that tingle.

It begins as a little ping and then gets increasingly worse, until it consumes your entire leg. Imagine both legs at the same time! I suffered in agony for several minutes as the blood flow slowly restored to my legs.

I don't judge the disciples anymore.

IT STILL COUNTS

Yes, I slept through my prayers. I had a prayer fail. Yet, because of my partnership with Jesus, God's mercy answered my prayers that night. Even as I snoozed my way to paralysis, Jesus stayed alongside me, praying at the right hand of the Father. The Spirit of Christ prompted me to get out of bed and pray in the first place, and the prayers of Christ continued while I dozed.

My heart was right; my eyes drooped with sleep. Still, Jesus covered me. I partnered with the Greatest Intercessor Ever. Whether the disciples realized it or not, they also partnered with Jesus in Mark 14:32–42. As they slept, Jesus prayed on.

Jesus knew about His imminent death. He understood the events soon to overtake Him. In that moment of deep sorrow and a heavy heart, Jesus prayed. He brought Peter, James, and John with Him to the garden with one request: "Stay here and keep watch" (vs. 34).

During the next hour while Jesus prayed, the disciples fell asleep. No doubt they made themselves as comfortable as possible while they waited, and then eventually dozed off. Three times. That had to be a little embarrassing. (But again, no judgment here.)

Jesus called them out, I suspect with both compassion and a little disappointment. "Couldn't you keep watch for one hour?" (vs. 37). Then He added a prophetic warning I doubt the disciples understood. He tied their sleepiness with a weakness toward temptation: "Watch and pray so that you will not fall into temptation. The spirit is willing, but the flesh is weak" (vs. 38).

He warned them about the power of prayer to sustain them in

the years ahead—and they had no idea how much they would need it!

Yes, the disciples failed miserably at staying awake on behalf of their friend. Yet, Jesus continued praying. With or without them, He remained fully present to His Father and interceded in His hour of great need. He prayed into the fullness of His destiny, and that of His disciples.

This can assure us today. Even as we slumber in our prayerlessness, or when evil lurks around us, ready to pounce on our weakness, Jesus prays for us.

Right now.

NECESSITY OF PRAYER

One question you might ask, and it's a valid one: "Did Jesus really need to pray?"

Here's my theologically profound answer: *Apparently, He did.*

Too many examples appear in Scripture to conclude anything else. Someone counted 45 times in the Gospels where Jesus went away to pray. It doesn't make sense that He would devote so much time to prayer if He didn't consider it a necessity for His life.

The Lord's prayer times didn't always focus on teaching or modeling intercession for others. In many instances, Jesus drew away to pray without anyone else present (Mt. 14:23; Lk. 5:16). We don't know what He prayed about during those times, and He didn't always reveal His intimate conversations with the Father. We just know it was important to Jesus that He orchestrate moments to be alone in prayer.

Other times, He modeled prayer, like instructing His disciples with The Lord's Prayer (Matt. 6:9–13). He also prayed at key moments—such as the resurrection of Lazarus—to benefit those around Him: "So they took away the stone. Then Jesus looked up and said, 'Father, I thank you that you have heard me. I knew that you always hear me, but I said this for the benefit of the people standing here, that they may believe that you sent me'" (Jn. 11:41–42).

We also notice that Jesus' prayers were often filled with emotion and agony. It's one more indicator that, yes, *Jesus needed to pray*: "During the days of Jesus' life on earth, he offered up prayers and petitions with fervent cries and tears to the one who could save him from death, and he was heard because of his reverent submission" (Heb. 5:7).

You can't study the life of Jesus without concluding that prayer was—and is—a critical component of His life. He modeled it, pursued it, and stayed impassioned about it. And now He intercedes at the throne of God: "Christ Jesus who died—more than that, who was raised to life—is at the right hand of God and is also interceding for us." (Rom. 8:34).

He is, after all, the Greatest Intercessor.

THE BIG ASK

As a young pastor's wife, Evelyn Christenson asked the Lord if she could teach the world to pray. She immediately repented of her request because she felt wrong making such a "big ask."

But the Lord spoke to her and said, *I'm the One who put the desire on your heart. So, ask Me!"*

Evelyn eventually traveled the world with speaking engagements and wrote several books on prayer, including a bestseller. Even though she passed away in 2011 at the age of 89, Christians in India still record and broadcast her materials. People in Nigeria and other countries read her books on evangelistic prayer. She really did teach millions around the world to pray!

Jesus taught about big-ask prayer as a model for how to ask with faith according to God's will:

- John 14:13–14. "And I will do whatever you ask in my name, so that the Father may be glorified in the Son. You may ask me for anything in my name, and I will do it."

- John 16:24. "Until now you have not asked for anything in my name. Ask and you will receive, and your joy will be complete."
- Matthew 7:7–11. "Ask and it will be given to you; seek and you will find; knock and the door will be opened to you. For everyone who asks receives; the one who seeks finds; and to the one who knocks, the door will be opened. Which of you, if your son asks for bread, will give him a stone? Or if he asks for a fish, will give him a snake? If you, then, though you are evil, know how to give good gifts to your children, how much more will your Father in heaven give good gifts to those who ask him!"

Jesus had a "big ask" Himself, one that His Father invited Him to pray. We read it in Psalm 2:7–8 (italics added):

> I will proclaim the Lord's decree:
> He said to me, "You are my son;
>   today I have become your father.
> *Ask me,*
> *and I will make the nations your inheritance,*
> *the ends of the earth your possession."*

Can you imagine a bigger ask? The Father instructed Jesus to ask for all the nations of the earth to belong to Him. This demonstrates one of the most significant encouragements about prayer that applies even to Jesus: *We need to ask.*

James affirms "you do not have because you do not ask God" (Js. 4:2). Don't miss this general principle of prayer that Jesus both instructed and implemented in His prayer life: *Don't be afraid to ask, even for the big things.*

HOW ELSE DID JESUS PRAY?

Jesus prayed other ways, too. The prayer concerns on His heart provide great clues for how we can pray, too.

- **Jesus prayed for God's direction.** When selecting the 12 disciples, Jesus prayed all night. We don't know the specifics of what He prayed, but we can at least imagine some requests on His heart: "Peter. He's going to have a rough go of it. Keep him and restore him." "Help Me to love Judas extraordinarily, because I know he will betray Me." "John is so young. Grow him up and prepare him for Kingdom assignments." I'm guessing Jesus asked not only for God's direction in His choice of disciples, but He also prayed for them in advance and dedicated them to God (Lk. 6:12–13).

- **Jesus prayed for others who needed God's forgiveness**. Despite Jesus' pain and impending death, He still communicated compassion and forgiveness for those who betrayed Him. "Jesus said, 'Father, forgive them, for they do not know what they are doing.' And they divided up his clothes by casting lots" (Lk. 23:34). Even when thirsty, bleeding out, and dying, Jesus knew the power of forgiveness. His prayer of forgiveness also applies to us when we fail to honor Jesus. His heart always forgives, and we receive the joy of restoration when we repent.

- **Jesus prayed for His beloved friends, and for followers to come**. Jesus' most lengthy recorded prayer pleaded for His disciples and believers in the future Church. He prayed prophetically, knowing His followers would always experience opposition from Satan. They would need to stay unified, so the world could witness the power and glory of Jesus (Jn. 17:1–26). Jesus still longs for His Church to love well and walk in power through unity in

Him. As His beloved, He prays for us even now, and we can join Him in this world-changing prayer.

This is not an exhaustive list of how Jesus prayed, but you can see through just a few examples that Jesus focused His prayers on others—and His heart is always for the advancement of God's Kingdom.

WHAT DOES JESUS PRAY NOW?

Jesus still fulfills His role as the Greatest Intercessor. It boggles the mind to think that right now He actively engages in intercession *on our behalf.* Hebrews 7:25 says He "always lives to intercede." You are never alone—even when you are not sure how to pray! Jesus *lives* to pray for you!

I like to joke that I practice "the gift of speculation." I enjoy pondering all the possibilities of a situation. (I'm not, however, particularly skilled at it!) But if you join me in my speculating, what do you think Jesus might be praying right now? Based on how He prayed on earth, what are some of the possible top prayers on His list?

- We will not fall away from the faith during trials. Instead, we will be conquerors (Lk. 22:32).
- We will remain in unity as followers of Christ (Jn. 17:20–23).
- We will love one another and love Christ (Jn. 13:34–35).
- We will be filled with the Holy Spirit, and marked by joy (Acts 4:31; 13:52).
- We will know the truth, embrace the truth, and walk in the truth (Jn. 17:17–19).

His prayer list most likely also includes these requests:
- He asks for the nations, praying for the greatest spiritual awakening and salvation harvest ever (Ps. 2:7–8).

- He advocates for us in the face of accusations from Satan, the accuser of the brethren. Satan says nasty and condemning things about us, and Jesus refutes it all because we belong to Him (Rev. 12:10).
- He advocates for us in our sin, so we will repent and reconcile to Him (1 Jn. 2:1).

OUR PARTNERSHIP WITH CHRIST

How does knowing that Jesus is interceding right now, affect your view about your own personal intercessory prayer time? Here are some ways I want my prayer life to be influenced by my partnership with Jesus:

- I want my prayers to line up with the ways Jesus prayed so that I can be certain I am praying according to God's will.
- I seek to invite Jesus, by the Holy Spirit, to lead me in how to intercede.
- I rest in those times when I don't know how to pray. Jesus already intercedes for me. I am not alone.
- I want to develop greater confidence to ask for the big things.
- I feel more honoring and respectful in my prayers because I realize Jesus and I approach the Father together.

REDEMPTION TIME

In the spring of 2017, I traveled to Israel. I never imagined myself visiting there, but God unexpectedly provided for me to make the trip with my pastor and friends from church. The sites and experiences solidified even more my confidence in the truth of God's Word.

As our group gathered on the Mount of Olives, we looked across the Kidron Valley to the walled parts of Jerusalem and the old city. We saw the approximate path Jewish leaders and a detachment of soldiers took as they headed toward the Garden of Gethsemane with their flaming torches in the night to seize Jesus. Obviously, Jesus clearly saw the mob coming toward Him. Yet Scripture says Jesus met them, even though He knew they intended to kill Him (Jn. 18:1–9).

It was a sobering time as we read Scripture, listened to our guide share historical facts, and then looked across the valley to where Judas betrayed Jesus. It was a holy moment. Then my pastor asked me to pray on behalf of our group. Okay, seriously, what a blessing and another profound moment!

Of course, I thought about the significance of Jesus' prayer in the Garden of Gethsemane. I remembered the disciples falling asleep in the shadow of His impending death. I recognized Jesus' agony and sacrificial love on behalf of His followers. I stood at one of the most sacred places in Israel, offering thanksgiving to Jesus for His incomparable sacrifice. I prayed with hope and anticipation for that glorious moment when He returns and the Mount of Olives splits in half with the power of His victorious presence (Zech. 14:4).

In that moment of prayer, I felt wide awake and thrilled to partner with my Jesus!

THINK ABOUT IT

Study Scripture passages to further represent the principles discussed in this chapter.

1. Read the big-ask verses in this chapter, and pull out additional prayer principles from John 14:13–14, 16:24, and Matthew 7:7–11.
2. Outline Jesus' prayer in John 17. List the ways He prayed. Then turn those concepts into points you can incorporate into your prayers.

PRAYER RESPONSE

Think about how to pray like Jesus. He is the best prayer example of all.

1. Practice praying like Jesus. Incorporate His examples into ways you pray for others. Imagine your partnership with Jesus. What example of His could you pray right now?

2. Ask Jesus to help you regularly follow His example in your prayer life. Tell Him the other ways you want to practice prayer like Him.

TIME TO MENTOR

Engage your mentees to explore the reality of Jesus praying with and for us. Invite them to think bigger about the content of their prayers. Their ideas might surprise and inspire you.

1. Ask your mentees to speculate about how Jesus prays right now at the right hand of the Father. Ask them to imagine the ways Jesus prays for His Church, for the lost, and for each mentee personally.

2. Review the big-ask Scripture passages in this chapter and relate times when you prayed boldly for specific needs.

3. If appropriate, ask each mentee to share the big request hiding in his or her heart. Discuss the barriers to big-ask prayer, and encourage everyone to pray for the seemingly impossible.

CHAPTER 7

Paul's Extraordinary Prayer Life

No one knows how to pray Kingdom prayers more than Jesus, who is both the Greatest Intercessor—and the One with all the answers!

But if we look for another biblical example of someone who knows how to approach the throne of God with passion, faith, confidence, and thankfulness, we can look to the prayer life of the apostle Paul. When Paul wrote his letters to the churches, he blessed us with examples of prayers for almost every occasion.

We could cover many topics of prayer according to Paul's examples, but in this chapter, we will touch on four: warfare prayers, prayer for all God's people, extraordinary love, and thankfulness.

THE REALITY OF WARFARE

I'm usually hesitant when a friend asks if I will edit his or her book. However, when my friend Mark asked me, I sensed I needed to make an exception. He wanted to write his life story, even if it never got published. He believed God led him to share his amazing transformation.

As I worked through Mark's book, his story shocked me. The Mark I knew now had dramatically changed from his life before meeting Christ.

In his early elementary school years, Mark felt jealous toward a classmate. In a boys-will-be-boys fashion, he planned to "get even" with this friend for all the attention he received from others. Mark invited the boy to play after school at a nearby creek. After a while, Mark pushed him into the creek, not realizing the current's danger. Before Mark could react, the water swept the boy down the creek and over a large waterfall. That was the last Mark saw of his classmate.

Mark returned home and told no one. People began searching for the child, and the police arrived at Mark's door to question him. Mark felt sure he would go to jail. Eventually, this scared little boy told the truth, and sadly, rescuers found his friend's body soon after.

When Mark returned to school, his classmates knew the story, and called him a murderer. This changed the trajectory of Mark's life. From that day on, he became an angry, hot-tempered little boy who challenged anyone who teased or wronged him. Some feared him as a vicious fighter. He felt like a monster and even worse, a murderer. His young identity was suddenly shaped in hopelessness.

Mark's anger carried into his adult life, causing a series of personal and relational issues. For years, he fought back angrily in his family, marriage, and business relationships. He hated himself and almost everyone else.

Then one day in 1996, a friend invited Mark to Promise Keepers, a conference for men, at the Major League baseball stadium in downtown Minneapolis. Mark walked into the venue as a broken man who felt no chance of redemption anywhere in his life. He and his friend arrived late and found seats only at the top of the stadium, far away from the stage.

Mark wrote about what a meaningless experience it was for him.

The sound system was terrible. He couldn't understand any of the words of the worship music or what the speakers were saying. It felt like a waste of time—that is, until the man who presented the gospel began to speak.

Suddenly, Mark heard every word perfectly. He listened to the message of salvation with clarity as the Spirit overwhelmed him. He put his head in his lap, wept tears of repentance, and gave his life to Jesus. In the light of the cross, he surrendered all the years of anger, bitterness, and self-hatred. That night, Jesus restored him.

FIRSTHAND WITNESS

When I read about Mark accepting Christ, emotion overcame me. I wrote a note to Mark in the margin of his book:

> Mark, I was in a locker room in the stadium that night, in the intercessor's prayer room. A leader came down and told us that the sound system was terrible and that the men could not understand the words, but that someone was about to get up to preach the gospel. So, they asked us to please pray for the gospel to be heard clearly. *Mark, I prayed for you that night!*

Almost 20 years later, editing Mark's book, I realized firsthand the power of prayer and the reality of spiritual warfare. I remember leaving the locker room to watch men stream forward to the stage to receive Christ. It was a spiritually thrilling moment. That night, God gave me a glimpse into the power of prayer and the warfare in the heavenly realms, especially around the clarity of the gospel.

Spiritual warfare swirls around us. That's reality. But we don't need to panic. We can learn to pray against it, standing firm and confident in the Lord. We can learn from the prayer life of the apostle Paul.

One of Paul's basic lessons from his prayer life addressed spiritual warfare. He instructed believers to stand guard against Satan's schemes and strategies because Jesus is our greatest weapon. Paul wrote about wearing the armor of God against spiritual onslaughts:

> Finally, be strong in the Lord and in his mighty power. Put on the full armor of God, so that you can take your stand against the devil's schemes. For our struggle is not against flesh and blood, but against the rulers, against the authorities, against the powers of this dark world and against the spiritual forces of evil in the heavenly realms. Therefore put on the full armor of God, so that when the day of evil comes, you may be able to stand your ground, and after you have done everything, to stand (Eph. 6:10–13).

In spiritual warfare, we can stand our ground when we employ all the elements of God's armor to equip us with the truth and righteousness of Christ, the message of the gospel, our active faith and sure salvation, and the Word of God by the power of the Spirit (Eph. 6:14–17). Paul taught the Ephesians—and us—to pray about everything and everyone, and to keep alert always: "And pray in the Spirit on all occasions with all kinds of prayers and requests. With this in mind, be alert and always keep on praying for all the Lord's people" (Eph. 6:18).

Then Paul pointed to the gospel, the reason we wrestle with the demonic realm. He asked for prayer, so he would not back down or feel intimidated as he shared the truths of Jesus Christ: "Pray also for me, that whenever I speak, words may be given me so that I will fearlessly make known the mystery of the gospel, for which I am an ambassador in chains. Pray that I may declare it fearlessly, as I should" (Eph. 6:19–20).

Paul's greatest concern involved spreading the gospel, fully aware Satan opposed him on all sides, including through people who gave themselves over to evil. He wrote: "As for other matters, brothers and sisters, pray for us that the message of the Lord may spread rapidly and be honored, just as it was with you. And pray that we may be delivered from wicked and evil people, for not everyone has faith" (2 Thess. 3:1-2).

When reading Paul's prayers about spiritual warfare, it is clear he didn't panic, fear, or get overwhelmed. He confidently prayed with the belief Jesus reigned stronger and greater than any evil force.

In his book *Christ Is NOW*, David Bryant emphasizes our need to keep our eyes on Jesus and His power to overcome warfare. He explains: "As we become increasingly passionate for Jesus the way the Father is, we will also experience more of His victory over powers of darkness. The Church secures triumphs by focusing fervently on who Christ is to us, not on what the devil throws at us."[5]

FALLING BOOKS

One evening when I walked from the garage into the lower level of my home, I noticed several books on the floor next to my bookshelf. *Strange,* I thought. I wondered what kind of vibration caused them to fall off the shelf. I returned the books to their places and headed upstairs. When I returned a few minutes later, the books lay on the floor again.

Okay, I thought, *that's for sure strange.*

I put them back on the shelf and sat down to watch television. Out of the corner of my eye, I saw the books fall off the shelf again. I can't explain my next reaction, except I felt confident in Christ's power and didn't feel afraid. Out loud, I spoke to a demonic spirit (I assume); I don't know how else to explain it. I said, "I'm going to finish watching this show, and I'll deal with you later."

It wasn't arrogance. I just felt certainty the power of Christ accompanied me. About an hour later, I replaced the books and then walked through my house, calmly telling any demonic spirits they held no right or authority in my home and must leave in the name of Jesus. I also prayed for the presence of Christ to fill my home and overpower evil. After that, no books fell, and I didn't feel intimidated in my home.

Yes, warfare exists, including the big confrontations and the annoying "smaller" incidents like falling books. Even so, we possess the greater weapons of prayer and the name of Jesus.

When Paul prayed, he didn't focus on the darkness. Likewise, he encouraged us to stay aware, keep our eyes fixed on Jesus, and root our prayers in His strength and power to overcome. Our best defense is grounding in the Word of God and invoking Jesus' name. We win battles through our posture of humility and the strength of His authority.

When you encounter what seems like a spiritual warfare, don't spend much time trying to figure out whether it's warfare or not. Just assume it is, humble yourself before the Lord, and call upon Him to strike fear in your enemies and scatter them by the power of His name.

PRAYER FOR ALL GOD'S PEOPLE

Joe was an elderly Jewish man who came to faith in Jesus, was rejected by his family, and became a part of the church fellowship where I attended right out of college. Probably in his 80s, Joe was an eccentric personality. He was stooped over and wore the same suit to church every week. He combined a vest, sweater, and suitcoat, and often stood up in the middle of a service to rearrange his layers, depending on whether he felt hot or cold. Sometimes he got tangled up in his clothes and needed help. Everyone knew at least once or twice during a service, Joe would distract the rest of us while he readjusted his vest and sweater.

Joe often called different members of the church to say he "needed a little fellowship." That meant he wanted a ride to church and would gladly give you the opportunity to buy him lunch.

A couple of friends and I decided to gather for prayer on Sunday nights, and chose a storage closet at the top of steep stairs over the baptistery. It felt like a cozy prayer closet to us.

Joe found out about it and insisted on joining us. You can probably picture us pulling and boosting him up those steep stairs. It felt like a labor of love and no doubt, it would have been easier to pray without him. But one thing about Joe, when he prayed, he was no novice. He clearly spent a great deal of time in God's presence.

When Joe needed to move to a new home, a friend and her husband agreed to help him. They figured he didn't own much furniture, so they rented a small trailer and pulled up to Joe's basement apartment. The husband went in to assess the situation. After a few minutes, the door opened, Joe walked out, and her husband followed him, carrying a suitcase. All his earthly possessions fit in that suitcase. No furniture. No bags of clothes. Just a suitcase.

I can name two things in that suitcase: Joe's Bible and the church directory. That's because Joe's greatest contribution to the Kingdom of God was prayer. He prayed through that directory, name by name, every week. His ministry revolved around praying for the saints, fellow believers in Christ who became his family. I am the recipient of many of Joe's prayers.

PAUL'S LOVE FOR THE SAINTS

Paul also spent considerable time praying for "the saints"—and he instructed the Church to do likewise. Paul loved the Church so well, and we learn from his example that the greatest way to show love is to pray for your fellow brothers and sisters in Christ.

In fact, in Paul's letters he prayed more for Christians than for people without Christ. He prayed for both, but Paul knew the importance of God's people staying strong in faith and passionate about advancing the Kingdom. Paul encouraged the Ephesians to "always keep on praying for all the Lord's people" (Eph. 6:18).

By looking at some of Paul's prayers for believers, we glimpse what Paul wanted for his co-laborers in Christ. These prayers can influence our prayers for brothers and sisters in Christ. Look at how Paul prayed for them:

- Strengthening of faith, an overflow of love, and increasing holiness. "Night and day we pray most earnestly that we may see you again and supply what is lacking in your faith. Now may our God and Father himself and our Lord Jesus clear the way for us to come to you. May the Lord make your love increase and overflow for each other and for everyone else, just as ours does for you. May he strengthen your hearts so that you will be blameless and holy in the presence of our God and Father when our Lord Jesus comes with all his holy ones" (1 Thess. 3:10–13).

- Endurance, encouragement, Christ-like attitudes, and unified voices giving glory to God. "May the God who gives endurance and encouragement give you the same attitude of mind toward each other that Christ Jesus had, so that with one mind and one voice you may glorify the God and Father of our Lord Jesus Christ" (Rom. 15:5–6).

- Wisdom and revelation to know God better, enlightened hearts, understanding the hope and riches in Christ, and embracing the incomparably great power. "I keep asking that the God of our Lord Jesus Christ, the glorious Father, may give you the Spirit of wisdom and revelation, so that you may know him better. I pray that the eyes of your heart may be enlightened in order that you may know the hope to which he has called you, the riches of his glorious inheritance in his holy people, and his incomparably great power for us who believe. That power is the same as the mighty strength he exerted when he raised Christ from the dead and seated him at his right hand in the heavenly realms, far above all rule and authority, power and dominion, and every name that is invoked, not only in the present age but also in the one to come" (Eph. 1:17–21).

• Worthy of His calling, spiritual fruit in good deeds, and the glory of Jesus in His people. "With this in mind, we constantly pray for you, that our God may make you worthy of his calling, and that by his power he may bring to fruition your every desire for goodness and your every deed prompted by faith. We pray this so that the name of our Lord Jesus may be glorified in you, and you in him, according to the grace of our God and the Lord Jesus Christ" (2 Thess. 1:11–12).

Many other Scripture passages exhibit how Paul prayed for Christ followers, but the wealth of prayer principles in these few verses bestow plenty of material for powerful, live-giving prayers for fellow believers. Your greatest contribution to the Kingdom of God may be your faithfulness in prayer for the saints.

Like Joe, we don't need much earthly reward if we focus on God's glory through His Church.

EXTRAORDINARY LOVE

Immediately upon graduating from college, I began my career as a journalist. I worked as an editorial assistant with a Christian magazine, which led to my future obsession with grammatically correct text messages and Facebook posts. God quickly immersed me into a world of journalism focused on writing and editing works related to prayer and advancing the gospel.

Soon after I received my first steady paycheck, I supported a friend in fulltime ministry. During one of her visits home after spending years overseas, she invited me for lunch to catch up.

As we finished our meal, she asked how she could pray for me. In that moment, I realized no one had ever asked me such a personal question. It seems like a normal thing now, but back then it marked a first for me, at least that I remember.

Without even thinking, I blurted out a response.

"I don't think I love people," I said.

My friend looked a little surprised.

"And when people say they love Jesus, I don't get what that means," I added. "I mean, I believe in Jesus as my Lord and Savior and want to serve Him, but I don't get the love part."

Now she looked stunned. In fact, she didn't respond. I guess when you say you don't love people and you don't know how to love Jesus, it has a quieting effect on the person across the table from you.

But it was a profound moment for me.

We said our goodbyes as we left the restaurant. I got into my car and sobbed. Voicing my feelings out loud uncovered something hidden deep within me. It started a journey of growing in love. I cried out to the Lord to change my heart, and to show me true love for Him and others.

God gradually softened my heart and put a love within me that altered my life. With that honest confession, I learned a critical prayer principle: *If you don't love, you really can't pray with the heart of God for others.*

PAUL'S DEEP LOVE

Paul felt extraordinary love for people. Desperate for them to know Jesus and His love, he wrote this:

> I speak the truth in Christ—I am not lying, my conscience confirms it through the Holy Spirit—I have great sorrow and unceasing anguish in my heart. For I could wish that I myself were cursed and cut off from Christ for the sake of my people, those of my own race, the people of Israel (Rom. 9:1–3).

We don't fully know what Paul meant by writing he'd rather be cursed and cut off from Christ for the sake of Israel's salvation. Scholars don't agree—and I certainly don't believe Paul meant he loved the Jews more than Christ. From what we know about Paul, he wouldn't choose anything other than Christ. But to express an extraordinary love, he described it in extreme terms. You can sense his agony, clarifying how desperately he loved and longed for lost people to know Jesus.

Full disclosure: I am not anywhere near Paul in my love for others. But I've come a long way since that lunchtime confession.

What would it be like to love like Paul did? Being cut off from Christ for the sake of another is not really an option. Salvation doesn't work that way. But what if we asked the Lord to give us that kind of supernatural love, motivated by a desperate desire for all people to know Christ's love?

Paul encouraged believers to pray this way: to let Christ shape extraordinary love in us. We can look at a couple of his prayers and allow them to shape our prayers:

And this is my prayer: that your love may abound more

and more in knowledge and depth of insight, so that you may be able to discern what is best and may be pure and blameless for the day of Christ, filled with the fruit of righteousness that comes through Jesus Christ—to the glory and praise of God (Phil. 1:9–11).

For this reason I kneel before the Father, from whom every family in heaven and on earth derives its name. I pray that out of his glorious riches he may strengthen you with power through his Spirit in your inner being, so that Christ may dwell in your hearts through faith. And I pray that you, being rooted and established in love, may have power, together with all the Lord's holy people, to grasp how wide and long and high and deep is the love of Christ, and to know this love that surpasses knowledge—that you may be filled to the measure of all the fullness of God (Eph. 3:14–19).

According to Paul, grasping Christ's love empowers us. When filled with Jesus' love—and His supernatural power—God can accomplish works beyond anything we can imagine (Eph. 3:20–21). This is a force that will change the world!

PRACTICAL LOVE

As I headed out of my apartment building for walk one spring day, I passed a woman in the lobby, waiting with her severely disabled child. The child uses a wheelchair and doesn't communicate. I've seen them before, and have always been cordial. As per usual, I said hello to the mom and headed outside.

I took just a few steps out the door when the Lord spoke to me. *You completely ignored that child.*

I stopped and felt compelled to turn around. I walked back in, knelt next to the child's wheelchair, and greeted her. I don't remember the words I spoke, but I engaged with her as best I could.

When I stood up, the mother asked me, "Do you still go to that church around the corner?"

I couldn't remember having a conversation with her about where I attend church. Perhaps she followed me out of the apartment lot one day, and watched me drive into the nearby church parking lot. I don't know how she made that connection.

"Yes, I do," I answered with surprise.

"Maybe we'll visit there some day," she replied.

A simple act of love speaks loudly. Sometimes, the opportunities stand right in front of us, if we stop to look and love.

Most likely, you can tell stories about pausing to show love and observing God at work because of your simple act. Love expressed in Christ is powerful, supernatural, and transformational. When we love well, it yields an audience. People pay attention, and perhaps, show an interest in Jesus.

Paul understood the power of love. I think God delights in a prayer for supernatural and extraordinary love, and He wants to answer it.

THANKFULNESS, ALWAYS

My mom gives thanks to God more than anyone I know. She praises Him for the weather, parking spaces, timing of phone calls, the food at her senior residence, and rides to church. There is nothing too small or insignificant for her to thank the God of the universe for His divine orchestration. She breathes thanksgiving.

Paul wrote about his thankfulness with the same enthusiasm, and focused on the greatness of God. Pay attention to the number of times Paul said, "Thanks be to God, I give thanks, or I always thank God." You can trace a pattern of gratitude.

Paul was a man overwhelmed with thankfulness because of his past, and for God's grace in his transformed life. He referred to himself as the worst of sinners (1 Tim. 1:15) and he continuously felt grateful that God still saw fit to redeem and use him for His glory.

Broken, redeemed people are thankful people.

Tremendous benefits and reminders affect us when we're thankful. Prayers that exude from a thankful heart:

- Remind us of how powerful God is.
- Remind us of His attributes and cause faith to arise in us.
- Remind us that in all circumstances, He loves us and works things out for His purposes.

When we focus on thankfulness and praise God for anything and everything, we bring our lives into alignment with His greater purposes. Apart from God, we're lost and doomed to a failed destiny. But when we cultivate gratitude, our souls prosper, and we keep our eyes fixed on the hope of Jesus.

Paul wrote wonderful examples of how to pray and thank God for key blessings in our lives. We can incorporate the apostle's scriptural prayers of gratitude into our own prayers:

- For God's grace, salvation, and riches in Christ Jesus. Paul could not stop thanking God for rescuing him from eternal damnation.

    I thank Christ Jesus our Lord, who has given me strength, that he considered me trustworthy, appointing me to his service. Even though I was once a blasphemer and a persecutor and a violent man, I was shown mercy because I acted in ignorance and unbelief. The grace of our Lord was poured out on me abundantly, along with the faith and love that are in Christ Jesus. Here is a trustworthy saying that deserves full acceptance: Christ Jesus came into the world to save sinners—of whom I am the worst. But for that very reason I was shown mercy so that in me, the worst of sinners, Christ Jesus might display his immense patience as an example for those who would believe in him and receive eternal life. Now to the King eternal, immortal, invisible, the only God, be honor and glory forever and ever. Amen (1 Tim. 1:12–17).

- For his co-laborers. Paul knew the importance of the Body of Christ. He loved the Church, and expressed thankfulness for fellow believers.

We always thank God for all of you and continually mention you in our prayers. We remember before our God and Father your work produced by faith, your labor prompted by love, and your endurance inspired by hope in our Lord Jesus Christ (1 Thess. 1:2–3).

- For those who touched his life or the lives of fellow believers. Paul was so grateful for people who loved well and encouraged each other in the faith.

We ought always to thank God for you, brothers and sisters, and rightly so, because your faith is growing more and more, and the love all of you have for one another is increasing. Therefore, among God's churches we boast about your perseverance and faith in all the persecutions and trials you are enduring (2 Thess. 1:3–4).

We always thank God, the Father of our Lord Jesus Christ, when we pray for you, because we have heard of your faith in Christ Jesus and of the love you have for all God's people (Col. 1:3–4).

A heart of thankfulness reframes everything. When we start our prayers with gratefulness to God, we remember His goodness, faithfulness, and love. It prompts us to confidently recall the graces bestowed upon us and to trust Him for the future.

Paul's great power resided in thankfulness, and he effectively employed that prayer strategy. Paul couldn't help himself. He had to say, "Thank You," to his gracious and merciful Father.

THINK ABOUT IT

From what you learned about Paul and his prayers, ponder and answer these questions.

1. Have you experienced spiritual warfare? How did you respond? What examples can you share with others?
2. Using scriptural examples from Paul's prayers, write a go-to prayer you can use for other believers. The point is not to create a rote prayer, but to begin thinking in biblical terms as you pray for others.
3. Choose a few Scripture passages from Paul's prayers that encompass your heart for brothers and sisters in Christ. Write them on cards or mark them in your Bible as passages you will pray consistently for others in your church, family, or friendships.
4. Conduct a deeper study on Paul's extraordinary love stated in Romans 9:1–3. Research what scholars write about this passage. Then, using Paul as a model, write your expression of love for others.

PRAYER RESPONSE

Pray about what you learned in this chapter. Pursue these prayers over several days. No need to hurry and accomplish them all at once.

1. Examine your prayer life. Spend a day noting how often you thank God for something. If you notice your gratitude lacking, intentionally thank God multiple times during your day. If you run into a friend in the store, thank Him for that friendship. After a day at the office, express thanksgiving for a job that provides for your family and uses your gifts and skills. Praise Him when you arrive home safely after time spent in traffic. Look at circumstances as a continuous opportunity to thank God.

2. List specific ways you can pray—even words or phrases—the next time you battle against dark spiritual forces. Ask Jesus to remind you of the power and authority of His name to make dark forces flee.

3. Perhaps you can't relate to Paul's extraordinary love. Tell the Lord the ways you struggle to love, and invite Him to work supernaturally in you. Remember, loving as Christ loves radiates from the Spirit. It's not something you can rally in your own strength.

4. Finally, list the people who've touched you in some way. Thank God for your parents, family and friends, people who pray for you, those who come alongside you in hard times, people who encourage you. Ask the Spirit to remind you of several people to add to your gratitude list. Name names and thank the Lord for their love and influence.

TIME TO MENTOR

Keep sharing with your mentees about your memorable prayer times and insights.

1. Think of times you experienced spiritual warfare, and how you prayed. Did you pray in confidence or struggle in fear? Spend time discussing warfare with your mentees. Explain your encounters

and listen to theirs. Help them grow in confidence to trust God and call upon Jesus' name.

2. Share ways you express thankfulness in prayer. Invite your group to pause and thank God for His blessings and for the godly people in their lives. Practice praying for all the saints.

CHAPTER 8

Just Do It: Radical Prayers

My friend Marty was discouraged. The surgeries on both of his arms were not successful, and he anticipated a summer of more surgeries and casts. As he relayed his story in a hallway conversation with me and a pastor, I felt a nudge to pray right then for his healing.

Unfortunately, I ignored the strong sense to pray in faith. I feared looking foolish, so I hesitated and let the opportunity pass. In my heart, I knew I disobeyed.

A few days later, Marty and a few friends gathered with me on a Friday evening to pray. We often met at the church late at night on weekends to pray for various ministries. As we knelt on the floor in an office, I remembered my disobedience a few days earlier.

"Marty," I said meekly, "God told me I was supposed to pray for your healing, and I didn't do it. I'm wondering if you will forgive me. And then I'm wondering if it would be okay if I pray right now before we pray for anything else."

Marty graciously forgave and invited me to pray for him. I then said one of my simplest prayers ever. I repented for my disobedience, and then asked, "God, will You please heal Marty's arms?"

That was it. There was nothing spectacular or profound about my prayer. It rose up from a repentant heart. We then prayed for other requests.

Later that night, as Marty drove home, he felt a crackling in his arms that caused him to pull over to the side of the road. He could feel the bones healing and correctly aligning themselves. Unnerved, Marty sat in his parked car for a long time, uncertain of what to do next. He wept and rejoiced, and then drove home.

On Monday morning, Marty kept his previously scheduled doctor's appointment. The doctor took x-rays of his patient's arms. After evaluating the film, he re-entered the examining room, astounded at the results. He brought along the previous x-rays and pointed out the difference to Marty. The bones in his arms were completely healed. In fact, the doctor felt so dumbfounded, he called other doctors in to review both sets of x-rays with him. Of course, Marty's explanation left the doctors admitting to a miracle.

Marty didn't need surgery, and after 20 years, his arms still work wholly and properly.

God impressed on me an important prayer principle through this healing. *Sometimes prayer is a matter of obedience, even when you don't necessarily have much faith.* Radical prayers are always appropriate, so go ahead and say them. "Pray away" because your hope lies in God alone to do the impossible.

YOU MIGHT BE THE CRAZY ONE

I admit sometimes I feel a little crazy. God calls me to unusual prayer assignments or activities, so I keep "under the radar." I'm not sure everyone will understand.

When living out a life of prayer, you'll eventually accept feeling like you're the crazy one. Sometimes, God might ask you to do or pray unexplainable things, but you're aware He has a purpose for asking you to intercede in an unusual or extraordinary manner.

My parents lived in the same house for 50 years in a small town in Minnesota. In many ways, small-town living helped shape my life and values. I could find my grandpa on any given morning at the local café, drinking coffee and eating donuts with his buddies. We could put our purchases on the tab at the grocery store, and I never hesitated to stop by the bank and chat with my dad in his office.

When my parents put their house on the market and moved to a senior living complex in a nearby, larger town, I grieved. As the community banker, my dad often helped people in crisis and led many to Christ in his office. The community loved and respected him. My mom also engaged with neighbors and townspeople, who knew her as a faithful prayer warrior. She never shied away from letting people know she prayed for them.

As we sorted through years of accumulation and packed up my parents' home, it felt like the end of an era. So, I decided to offer one last prayer blessing to the town. I prayerwalked every street and prayed for a Christ-awakening in each home. It took a few weekends of traveling back to the town and mapping out a route to walk, but I managed to finish praying for every home, business, and church before moving my parents. My overarching prayer asked that revival and spiritual awakening would transform the town of Brownsdale.

Imagine my surprise several months later when the town's Facebook page posted items like, "Revival and healing is on its way," and, "Brownsdale needs a time of refreshing." The posts were promoting an event sponsored by the local Baptist church, a weekend of music and preaching under a large tent called the Red Rock Revival. Granted, I prayed for a more of a supernatural, all-encompassing revival and spiritual awakening, touching the entire town with Christ's presence. Still, I took these online announcements as great encouragement that

God prompted me to pray the prayers He one day intended to answer.

A couple years later, I came across the Facebook page of that same church, and noticed the pastor gave his resignation due to health problems. I only met the pastor once, but I messaged him, thanking him for how he'd encouraged the town. I mentioned stories I'd heard about his kind and gentle spirit, and how he ministered to people.

He messaged back right away and said he'd purchased hundreds of the *Jesus Film Project* DVDs (produced by Cru) to pass out to every home in the community. The video tells the story of Jesus' life and presents the gospel message. As his final act of love before he retired and moved away from the town, he hoped to walk door to door with the truth of Jesus. It wasn't hard to "connect the dots" that perhaps a Christ-awakening in every home was headed that way.

Sometimes with radical prayer, you proceed with whatever God prompts you to do, but you may not receive the answer in your lifetime. Or maybe you will. Obedience doesn't demand an outcome; it just offers a heart to be used of God.

If God calls you to pray and it seems crazy to others, well, join the club. Many crazy, obedient God-followers appear in Scripture. Let's look at some of them. Read the following passages and write the "crazy" prayer in the provided spaces.

• **Joshua.** Read Joshua 10:1–15. His prayer:

_____

_____

_____

Did Joshua understand all the dynamics and physics of our solar system to realize what it would take for God to make the sun "stand still" until the battle ended? Probably not. However, Joshua most likely knew the consistent sun and moon patterns that determined many Jewish Festivals. Joshua asked God for something impossible that never happened in his lifetime. But that didn't matter. He just needed God to come through, so he prayed a bold, courageous, crazy prayer. Apparently, God didn't hesitate to rearrange laws of physics in answer to Joshua's prayer.

Don't overthink your prayers based on the probability of God answering them. If God leads you to say a crazy, obedient prayer, you might need to suspend any anticipated outcome. Just pray, and leave everything else to God's infinite wisdom and purposes.

- **Elijah.** Read 1 Kings 18:20–39. Elijah's prayer:

_____

_____

_____

Elijah uttered one of my favorite prayers in Scripture. It's to the point, direct, and confident. Elijah felt so sure he obeyed God, he didn't hesitate to say a radical prayer. Elijah set up God to prove Himself with a blaze of fire from heaven, and the prophet even included a request for God to validate his obedience.

God honored Elijah's bold prayer with a firestorm, defying any laws of nature. When we say radical prayers, we honor God with our belief in His power.

At one point during my trip to Israel, my pastor invited me to read this prayer passage from 1 Kings 18 as we stood on Mount Carmel. He had no idea how profoundly Elijah's prayer influenced my faith journey, and this created a memorable moment for me. I quoted the prayer close to the spot where Elijah most likely prayed it. That felt like a crazy and radical "coincidence," but God knew I would love it.

- **Elijah, again.** Now read another crazy story in 1 Kings 18:41–45. How did Elijah pray? Write out his prayer, and describe his posture and confidence in radical prayer:

_____

_____

_____

I refer to Elijah's prayer for rain as "revival praying." He saw nothing, nothing, nothing, nothing, nothing, nothing, and then *everything* in a mighty downpour! It takes a radical heart of faith to pray for revival year after year with no evidence of God moving. But when He does, it changes everything.

People may not understand your persistence in praying for revival in a seemingly hopeless world, but don't give up. Stay radical. Stay hopeful. Perhaps one day you will feel the downpour from heaven.

- **Elisha.** Read 2 Kings 6:11–18. Copy Elisha's prayer, and the outcome:

_____

_____

_____

Elisha's relationship with the Lord was so intimate, God revealed to him everything the king said in his private bedroom. Think about that for a moment. Nothing is hidden from God, and He can reveal anything to His servants for His purposes.

In a moment of complete calm, Elisha prayed a simple

prayer. He asked for his servant to be able to see in the spiritual realm. This is a radical, yet confident prayer. And God granted his request so that Elisha's servant could be encouraged about God's power.

Perhaps you've prayed for God to open a friend's eyes to the unseen spiritual world. It's a powerful prayer because it's the truth, as crazy as it may seem!

OBEDIENCE CAN BE COSTLY

Perhaps you've heard the story about the assistant football coach from a high school in Washington who kneeled in the center of the field at the end of games. Players could voluntarily join him, but he never asked or directed anyone to do so. The school administration told the assistant coach he could pray privately in a classroom or press box, but not on the field. No doubt, he sought God about what to do, and he continued his seven-year tradition of praying. Members from both teams prayed with him as a show of support.

As you can guess, the administration fired the assistant coach. Radical, humble, public prayer can be costly.

Scripture includes examples of the sometimes costliness of radical prayer. Think of Daniel, his insistence to pray daily, and his encounter with lions. Or let's consider a queen and her life-and-death costly prayer.

• **Esther.** Read Esther 4:15–17; 6:1-3. Esther's prayer:

_____

_____

_____

When Esther realized the annihilation of the Jews was imminent, she didn't hesitate to forge a radical prayer quest. She instructed the Jews in her kingdom to pray and fast on her behalf for three days, as she prepared to approach the king to ask for favor. Fully aware of violating the law, she declared, "If I die, I die" (4:16). But she also knew perhaps God raised her to the position of queen "for such a time as this" (vs. 16).

As a result of the Jews' desperate prayers and radical obedience in fasting, the king couldn't sleep. So, late at night, a servant read records of the ruler's reign to him. The king discovered Mordecai protected his life from assassins, and set into motion God's divine plan to expose Haman's jealous rage and evil plot against Mordecai and the Jews. The king granted Esther to speak with him, and God reminded the king to honor Mordecai, and thus, save the Jews.

Obedience in prayer can cost you, but God will work His purposes through your submission. Perhaps it's a test of what you're willing to do, and He will grow and strengthen your faith. Or perhaps it could save a family or a nation!

BECAUSE-YOU-SAY-SO PRAYERS

Sometimes we need to pray and act with radical obedience simply because Jesus says so. He drops the idea in our hearts, so we pray. Drawn from Scripture, we obey the Lord and respond, "because You say so."

- **Peter.** Read Luke 5:1–11. Write out Jesus' instruction and Peter's response:

_____

_____

_____

Peter and his friends fished all night with no results. Zero fish. Yet Jesus told Peter to throw out his nets another time. It made no sense, and probably grated against Peter's fishing instincts. No doubt, Peter looked foolish in front of his fishing buddies. But Peter cast his nets again for one reason alone. He responded to the Lord, "Because you say so" (vs. 5).

The result of Peter's say-so response? His nets broke from the abundance of fish! Jesus overwhelmed Peter with His majesty, power, and sovereignty.

You might sense God leading you into prayer assignments that make no sense. It could go against everything you think about a situation. Still, God asks you to pray with a different spiritual reality: with Him alone, all things are possible.

Years ago, I joined a prayerwalking group directed by God to research the history of North Minneapolis, and then boldly enter a crime- and poverty-ridden part of our city to pray for God's restoration of the rampant brokenness.

We researched through articles and historical documents about the origin of prostitution in North Minneapolis. We discovered the approximate corner where police identified prostitution and made the first arrest decades ago. Even though it seemed a bit radical, and perhaps somewhat hopeless in such a dark place, we piled into cars and drove to the spot.

When we stepped out of our cars in front of a house on that corner, we noticed a speaker attached to the house, blaring Christian music into the street. That encouraged us. As we gathered in a circle on the corner and prayed, a car pulled up. A woman got out and suspiciously asked, "What are you doing in front of my house?"

We explained we discovered prostitution began on her corner, and were there to pray for God's redemption. She began to weep.

Through tears, the woman shared she'd lived on this corner—feeling completely alone—for more than 30 years. She knew God assigned her to stay in a failing neighborhood and pray. She couldn't believe God sent in reinforcements to bless her, confirm her calling, and stand with her.

The woman knew nothing about her neighborhood's history; that prostitution started on her corner. She pointed to a freeway sound-barrier wall across from her house, where she'd posted a handwritten sign: "No guns, no gangs, no prostitution." She remained and prayed, taking a stand for the Lord on her corner because Jesus said so.

That's the essence of obedient prayer, even when you feel a bit crazy. If God puts something in your heart, you need only one response: "Yes, Lord, because You say so."

THINK ABOUT IT

Have you prayed because the Lord said so? If not, how do you feel about the possibility? Think about this as you explore the following questions.

1. Write about a time when you thought you heard the Lord—and then wondered if you actually heard Him ask you to pray in a certain way. How did you respond? What was the result?

2. Describe your current level of faith and how it might impact your prayer. Are you radical, or fearful and paralyzed? List some steps you can take to grow more confident in your prayer life.

3. Are you willing to pray because God says so? How can you identify His voice, asking you to pray in an unusual way?

PRAYER RESPONSE

An effective prayer life often involves asking God what to pray for people or circumstances. Use today's prayer response to ask God to help you pray big.

1. Ask the Lord whether He wants you to pray some crazy or radical way. Maybe it's to prayerwalk around your neighborhood or in a struggling part of your community. Perhaps you're to pray out loud for healing for a non-believing family member in his or her presence. It could be anything. Ask the Lord if He is inviting you to be obedient in something. Then just do it!

2. Pray for opportunities to encourage others to join you in radical prayer. Ask God to help you get over the fear of being the crazy one.

TIME TO MENTOR

Take the principles of this chapter to your mentor group. Perhaps you'll stir up crazy ways for each member to pray.

1. Read all this chapter's Scripture passages with your mentor group. In light of these verses, discuss the risks and rewards of radically obedient prayer.

2. Describe an incident when you risked and prayed in a radical way. How did you feel? What was the outcome?

3. In what ways could group members practice radical prayer? Ask if they sense God leading them to pray because He says so. Pray together about these possibilities.

CHAPTER 9

Back to the Basics

Perhaps you recall my story about how my prayer life was paralyzed for a short time when someone confronted me with the accusation, "You pray wrong!" For a few days, I believed the lie that if my prayers were not perfectly crafted and carefully worded, I was ineffective and a poor model for others.

In later years, as I've mentored others in prayer, perhaps one of the most important lessons I share is not to be intimidated or feel inadequate in your prayer life because of your comparison with others. God has wired you uniquely to pray and seek Him. He delights in hearing your voice—whether you pray with confidence and boldness (and a little extra volume) or in a soft voice that is intimate and personal. It is not about your style or wordsmithing of the perfect prayer. It is about the heart of one who is humble and dependent on the Lord for all things.

Ultimately, God desires the heartfelt cries of *someone* who is willing to invite Him to bless, protect, heal, restore, intervene, deliver, and bring Christ-transformation to our world.

My friend Tanya found a large, flat rock in her yard and turned it into a decorative prayer reminder that now sits on my living-room floor. She painted one of my favorite intercession verses on the rock:

I looked for *someone* who might rebuild the wall of righteousness that guards the land. I searched for *someone* to stand in the gap in the wall so I wouldn't have to destroy the land, but I found no one (Ezek. 22:30, NLT, italics added).

This verse encourages me. To me, it says God isn't picky about who steps up to the plate. He simply looks for someone with a righteous heart, willing to intercede and plead with Him on behalf of others. It's more about living right before God than the right words.

My pastor, Dr. Bob Bakke, often preaches on prayer because it's his heartbeat. He says God calls forth His people to stop His judgment. Essentially, the Lord calls out, "*Somebody* stop Me, that I might be gracious and pour out My mercy!"

AN INTERCESSOR'S ASSIGNMENT

Intercession, in its simplest definition, means praying on behalf of, interceding, for another. Your assignment as a Christ-following intercessor is to "be the one" to ask God to display His grace, love, mercy, and glory to our world.

God calls all believers to intercession. It's not an optional assignment, but an act of obedience to seek Him in prayer on behalf of others. However, I do believe God especially equips some people and fills them with passion to intercede beyond the usual discipline of prayer. These intercessors feel compelled to pray at levels of persistence and faithfulness perhaps other believers don't sense. The Spirit moves them in a specific way as they exercise the blessing of intercession. You know who they are; you can name them.

Yet, we're all called to a lifestyle of prayer. Through intentionality and practice, prayer becomes a natural part of our days, as natural and rhythmic as breathing. The more we practice prayer, the more it develops into our first response to every situation. Paul describes it like this: "And pray in the Spirit on all occasions with all kinds of prayers and requests. With this in mind, be alert and always keep on praying for all the Lord's people" (Eph. 6:18).

Effectiveness in the Kingdom of God depends on walking in a lifestyle of prayer. What occupies your thoughts as you drive around town, or take a coffee break at the office, or traipse through the grocery store, or clean up after your family's dinner? Do you fill your thoughts with prayers for others? I recall a time walking through the aisles of a store in search for an item, not realizing that I was also urgently praying and saying, "Jesus, Jesus, Jesus" out loud as I went up and down the aisle. I later thought if anyone heard me, I wanted to explain I was praying and not using my Lord's name in vain!

WHY BOTHER TO PRAY?

"Much prayer, much power. Little prayer, little power. No prayer, no power." That's a quote attributed to different people, including E.M. Bounds. I grew up hearing it often from believers passionate about missions. Even with uncertainty about the quote's origin, it's packed with truth. Power in ministry directly correlates to faithfulness in prayer.

I've spent many late nights praying with friends for God's movement in our church. It's always a joy to pray with Madan, a friend who grew up as an "untouchable" in India, but accepted Christ through a Swedish missionary. He preaches the gospel to tens of thousands of people when he travels back to India. He's challenged our little prayer group many times to remember who we pray to and why. God spoke clearly to Madan one night in his personal prayer time and reminded him, "I am *big*. Respect Me!"

When Madan shared this truth with us, it restructured how we prayed. We respect God and pray believing in all His attributes:

power, majesty, glory, sovereignty, rule, control, authority, and more. If we really believe in His "bigness," we will invoke much prayer with much power.

Yet, we struggle with prayer. We believe in its importance, but we lack consistency and intentionality. We can easily fall into a mind-set of "Why bother?"

Why does this happen? Let me suggest a few reasons why we *don't* pray. Perhaps something on my list will resonate with you:

• *We resign ourselves to "whatever will be, will be."* We feel long-standing discouragement over unanswered prayer, and we grow resigned to a seemingly impossible plight. We lose our passion and fervor to pray because there doesn't seem to be a point to asking for something that never changes. We give up and move on.

• *We hold an inadequate view of God and His willingness to work in answer to prayer.* I often hear people say, "Well, it must be God's will," when prayer disappoints them. Rather than pursue God like the persistent widow in Luke 18:1-18, they default to unanswered prayer as what God intends for them. They lose their fire and passion to keep on asking, seeking, and knocking as Jesus instructed in Matthew 7:7-8. God invites us to "annoy Him" with our continuous asking for desires buried deep within our hearts.

• *We're paralyzed with fear and unbelief.* We predetermine the outcome of our prayers by paralyzing ourselves with doubt. What if God doesn't answer? What if I put myself out there in a flurry of faith and belief, only to feel foolish with no response? What if I take the risk, and get disappointed once again? I've wrestled with these thoughts, yet I still migrate to this basic truth: I can't *not* pray! As often as I struggle with prayers not answered the way I anticipated, I'm fully convinced I've no other option but to keep praying.

- *We're just plain lazy.* Let's admit it. It feels like too much work. It's easier to relax on the couch and watch television than to excuse ourselves to pray fervently in another room. God calling us into fasting or another kind of sacrificial prayer doesn't fit with our weekend plans. We want answers, but not with a cost attached. Sometimes we treat God like a vending machine: we plug in a prayer and get the preferred answer. We're affected by a culture that invests little, but expects great returns.

- *We battle an enemy who delights in our distractions.* Prayer is war. We're in a battle for the glory of Christ to reign and for lost souls to awaken to salvation through Him. Satan and his demonic hoards will distract us in any way possible. Destroying our prayer lives tops his battle plan. Fortunately, we can identify Satan's schemes and strategies and fight against him (2 Cor. 2:11).

I suspect from time to time, most of these reasons affect our fervency and faithfulness in prayer. When you're stymied, remember the struggle is real. God calls intercessors to band together and influence the course of history to the glory of God.

TIME TO STEP UP

By contrast, given our God-ordained roles of intercession, let's review reasons we *should* pray:

- *There's no hope apart from prayer.* I'm increasingly desperate for the Lord to move powerfully and break through the bondages, strongholds, sin, and complacency in my life and in others. I can't imagine the hopelessness of a world without the gift of prayer. No matter how discouraged I get with the state of our nation, or the rebellious nature of people around me, I still hope at some point God will break through in answer to my prayers. I like to keep believing that perhaps, just perhaps, the next prayer I offer will ignite a breakthrough moment.

- *Others need us to pray.* Many people feel uncertain about how to seek God. It's possible nobody has ever prayed for them personally. I remember stopping by a friend's house to visit and listen to her story about marriage struggles within her family. I stopped right then and prayed for her. I think it surprised her. While some of us frequently pray on the spot, others feel taken back by the love and care shown by someone who prays for them immediately. Later, my friend sent a message, asking me to pray for another situation. As followers of Jesus, we can say, "I'll pray for you. Don't be afraid to ask me."

- *God needs us to pray.* Remember Ezekiel 22:30: God looked for someone to stand in the gap, so He would not destroy the land. This partnership is hard to comprehend, yet God designed a transformational relationship between us and Him. Does He really need us? Perhaps it's better to say He chooses to work both in and through us. My pastor often says, "Without Him, we can't. Without us, He won't." God chooses to make us a critical part in the equation of His power at work.

Yes, we can struggle with a consistent and faith-filled prayer life. One of my greatest encouragements in prayer occurs in relationships with others. When I pray with friends, whether in a small group or over the phone, I feel strengthened and encouraged to keep pressing on. Jesus indicated prayer isn't a go-alone battle. In Matthew 18:20 He reminded His followers: "For where two or three gather in my name, there am I with them."

If you feel lacking in your prayer life, call up some friends. Set a time to pray together. Let the presence of Christ—and the joy of fellow believers—keep you seeking and fully engaged in prayer.

PRAYER TAKEAWAYS

As I mentioned before, I'm more of a prayer practitioner. I practice, fail, practice, succeed, oops—fail, and then practice more at prayer. You can practice, too, applying your strengths and lessons in prayer, and pass them on to others. I hope in the back of this book, you also continue journaling your stories and best prayer practices.

As a review, the following prayer takeaways might refresh your memory about how God worked in your prayer life. As you read through these principles, note God's lessons to you, and thoughts you can pass on to others.

- **Don't lose heart.** Jesus used the example of the persistent widow in Luke 18:1–8 to give us permission to stay annoying and persistent in prayer. He invited us to ask again and again. And again and again. We don't know what could happen between our "asks" and His response, but we're not to give up. If you still carry a burden on your heart or struggle with an unresolved issue, don't quit. If you don't sense a release in your spirit, then keep praying. Pray like you're just one prayer away from an astounding answer.

- **Could You please show up?** Elijah put God on the line with a radical display of faith (1 Kings 18:36–37). In front of hundreds, perhaps thousands, he asked God to send down fire from heaven.

He determined that everyone would know his God as the one and only God. Do your prayers reflect a confidence in the only true God? Yes, it's risky to our pride to put God on the line. But someone who lacks confidence or hope in God may need to hear you pray with a determination and desire for God to show His glory and power.

- **Nothing, nothing, nothing ... everything**! Prayer for revival can continue for years before God shows up. Or, He can pour out His Spirit in an instant. We don't know His timetable. But remember Elijah in 1 Kings 18:41–45: He prayed seven times, with his face to the ground in desperate, groaning prayer until God sent the rainstorm. You might pray and see nothing, nothing, nothing. But eventually you will see everything: the glory of Christ displayed in all its brilliance. Perhaps it will be a preview now in our day through a move of revival and spiritual awakening, or perhaps it will be full-blown at Jesus' return. But be assured *every prayer counts*. Every time you ask for God's glory to be made known, that prayer counts for eternity.

- **For survival's sake.** Satan, our enemy, tries to destroy and kill us. Jesus instructed in Mark 14:34, 38 to keep watch always and pray to avoid temptation. He also warned in Luke 21:36 that persecution, destruction, and the end of times will come, so keep watch and pray. We're called as watchmen—and women—to pray. Historically, watchmen filled two primary purposes: to guard the city fields from thieves or prey, and to warn of an impending attack on the city. When we pray, God opens our eyes with what the spiritually blind cannot understand. We must stay alert in prayer to all threats. Our survival—and that of others—depends on it.

- **This is war!** We may not see into the heavenly realms, but a cosmic battle rages around us. In Daniel 10, we read about Daniel's faithfulness to fast and pray for 21 days before he encountered a man whose face looked like lightning and his voice roared like multitudes. Daniel fell on his face like a dead man. He also learned that while he prayed, the angel Gabriel and archangel Michael battled the demonic prince of Persia. Daniel's humble prayers ignited a spiritual wrestling match with eternal consequences. God might never reveal the engagement of war in the heavenly realms as you pray, but rest assured you're strategic in His plan.

- **Favor, plus some.** Nehemiah felt burdened to rebuild the broken-down walls of Jerusalem (Neh. 1:4–10; 2:4–5, 7–9). He didn't simply pull together a building committee and devise a plan. Nehemiah first prayed, repented, fasted, mourned, and asked God to give him favor with the king. In response, God provided Nehemiah with everything he asked for, plus some. The king gave Nehemiah the supplies he needed, and threw in men to guard the prophet's expedition. We're the spiritual repairers of walls in our cities, but we need to humble ourselves and ask the Lord for favor to accomplish everything for His glory. When you pray, ask for what you need, and don't be surprised when God blesses you above and beyond—just because He can.

- **Moment of desperation.** Jehoshaphat was a desperate man. Enemies surrounded his people, and he couldn't envision a hopeful solution (2 Chron. 20). He prayed the words of a desperate man: "We do not know what to do, but our eyes are on you" (vs. 12). God's answer to Jehoshaphat's humble cry essentially said, "Don't worry about it; just worship Me. I'll take care of your

115

enemies" (vs. 15-17, paraphrased). We can feel panic when life closes in, our enemies surround us, and it appears we have no hope. God invites us to cry out to Him. He wants to hear our voices when we desperately lean into Him.

- **This is not as good as it gets.** One of the most hopeful prayer passages in Scripture is 2 Chronicles 7:14: "If my people, who are called by my name, will humble themselves and pray and seek my face and turn from their wicked ways, then I will hear from heaven, and I will forgive their sin and will heal their land." It's a promise to Israel, but it indicates God's character and willingness to answer the prayers of humble people who repent and seek His face. When we meet God's conditions of humility, repentance, and looking to Him alone, His loving nature responds with forgiveness and the healing of our land. The exact nature of the healing looks different in every situation. But you can count on this truth: God wants to display His glory if we seek Him and ask. Whatever your family or church or city—or even your nation—looks like now, you don't need to live with a hopeless this-is-as-good-as-it-gets mentality. Don't let that lie dead-end your prayer life. Always pray with hope for healing and restoration.

SO, WE KEEP PRAYING

A few years ago, a friend published a story in her church publication about a woman who received a miraculous healing. I was so taken with the story, I asked my friend to rewrite it for *Prayer Connect* magazine.[6] Personally, it became one of my go-to stories when I needed—and still need—encouragement to keep praying about what seems impossible.

Ema McKinley suffered from Reflex Sympathetic Syndrome (RSD) after a workplace accident a few decades ago. It left her wheelchair bound with a twisted spine. In Rochester, MN, people dubbed Ema "the crooked lady" because of the unusual way her body leaned sideways in the wheelchair. She received the best medical expertise through the Mayo Clinic in her hometown, but no cure for her condition existed. She lived in burning pain, swelling, skin sensitivity, and sleep deprivation, along with her twisted spine, hand, and foot.

Over the years, many people prayed for Ema's healing. The elders of her church prayed for her. Ema also sought God to intervene during almost 20 years of agony. Yet, even without an answer to her most deeply held desire, Ema stayed faithful to prayer. It was difficult to attend church because of the great effort to get inside, but she often asked the driver of her wheelchair-equipped van to park outside the church, so she could pray for the pastors and the people.

One Christmas Eve, alone in her home, Ema reached for something and accidently fell out of her wheelchair. She sprawled on the floor, helpless to get up on her own. She laid on the floor for more than eight hours in extreme pain, praying and wondering if her time to die had finally come.

Suddenly, she felt the powerful presence of God. She described it as God entering her body. In amazement, she watched her twisted foot straighten out, and then her curled and useless hand opened up. The raw skin inside her hand healed before her eyes.

Then she felt God's healing work begin on her neck and spine. Suddenly she found herself flipped over on her back. She could feel the healing going through her entire body. And then, as she describes it, she saw the white robe of Jesus as He knelt beside her—and helped her to stand up. For the first time in two decades, Ema walked!

She decided to surprise her children and grandchildren the following morning when they came for Christmas. She left her empty wheelchair by the door—and then shocked her family as she walked down the hallway toward them. This astounding miracle left her

Mayo doctors without any natural explanation.

Ema wrote a book, *Rush of Heaven,* and appeared on news programs and talk shows. Nobody could deny the miraculous work of God in her life.

She prayed for healing for years, but Ema also trusted God in His wisdom, timing, and sufficient grace. In the same way, we don't know if or when God might answer miraculously on this side of heaven, blessing us and proclaiming His glory. But we must stay faithful in prayer.

LET'S CRAWL!

Many times, God uses a story to remind me of His power, loving nature, and unlimited ability to answer any prayer I offer. When I get overwhelmed by my struggles and don't know how to pray, an answered-prayer story can remind me to *pray big!* I have no idea when years of crying out might result in an instantaneous moment of God's powerful, restoring presence.

Don't give up. Don't feel intimidated. Remember the stories of Scripture. Remember your stories and those of others. Rely on the promise of Romans 8:26 and pray with hope:

> In the same way, the Spirit helps us in our weakness. We do not know what we ought to pray for, but the Spirit himself intercedes for us through wordless groans.

You're not alone. This is a team effort. It's you, the Holy Spirit, Jesus, and all of us as the Church together.

So, go and multiply yourself. The next generation needs an infusion of faith and belief. You can always mentor someone in prayer. Maybe it's a group of people, perhaps it's a child. Maybe it's a friend who needs to encounter Jesus in a personal way. You have a lifetime of experiences to share, much encouragement to offer.

Crawl under the stage with me. Tell your stories. Pray like you believe it. And if you listen carefully, you can hear the voices of the next generation rising to take their place in God's Kingdom.

THINK ABOUT IT

Before you close this book, think about your ability to mentor others, and prepare to step into an adventure. Don't discount your experience or preparation. Uncover how your life has prepared you for prayer mentoring.

1. Be honest. List the reasons you don't think you can mentor the next generation.
2. Now refute each of those reasons with what you've learned in this book and through Scripture.
3. Who could you possibly mentor in prayer? Pray about asking them to participate in a mentor group. Also, ask God to bring spiritually hungry mentees to you.

PRAYER RESPONSE

Turn your prayer response toward mentoring others to pray. The Lord will honor your desire and efforts to teach others about talking to Him.

1. Ask the Lord to transform your thinking about your role as an intercessor and a mentor. If you've limited yourself or discounted your ability to mentor, surrender that to the Lord. Ask Him to increase your faith and understanding of prayer, and instill a vision to pass on your prayer experiences to others, especially the next generation.
2. Write a prayer that expresses your desire to move ahead in prayer—and prayer mentoring—with God.

TIME TO MENTOR

More than you know, you're probably equipped to prepare others—for prayer, mentoring, and a lifetime of watching God work.

1. Encourage your group to list struggles in prayer. Learn from and encourage one another. Let mentees know that everyone struggles, and God still hears and answers those prayers.

2. What are your best prayer practices? List the variety of ways you've learned to pray. Share these with your mentor group, inviting them to add their prayer experiences to the list. God welcomes a variety of prayer expressions, so invite Him to lead you in fresh and creative ways.

3. Encourage your mentees to pray about becoming mentors. Explore their abilities, preparation, and experiences with them. Mentees might not realize God has already equipped them for this role.

How to Use the Handouts

The following handouts are designed to help you as a mentor by high-lighting key points and Scripture passages from each chapter. If you are teaching from this book, you can refer to these pages, copy them, or reproduce the handouts on 8½ x 11 sheets of paper so your mentees can take notes. Each handout includes a prayer assignment for mentees to experience with a prayer partner.

One

ANSWERING A HEART-RACING CALL

God calls us to the privilege of prayer, but sometimes we don't feel very good at it. Explore your prayer life and stories. You might be surprised at what you discover.

1. What is your prayer story? Do you feel somewhat experienced or completely intimidated in prayer? Growing up, did certain incidents or teachings shape you? Is there someone in your life who encouraged you in prayer? Write your story.

_____

_____

_____

_____

_____

_____

2. Regarding prayer, what are your joys, struggles, or fears?

   • Joys. How have you watched God at work because of prayer?

_____

_____

_____

- Struggles. List your struggles, such as a consistent prayer time, faith to believe in the power of prayer, and others.

- Fears. Do you harbor fears about prayer? List some of them, such as fear of praying wrong, not having the right words, fear of praying out loud, and others.

Your Prayer Assignment. Do you recall personal stories of answered prayer? Or times when you felt encouraged in prayer? Begin a journal of prayer experiences. Pray and ask God to bring stories to mind. Write about times when God increased your faith in the power of prayer. You can use the journal at the back of this book, or your own. Refer to your journal each week, and add the lessons you learn.

Two

PICK A PERSONALITY

Our personalities, temperaments, and prayer styles figure into how we intercede. God will stretch us in our prayer lives, but you probably practice the way you feel most called to pray.

Read the following Scripture passages and write down everything you notice about each person's personality: how the person prayed, and how it characterized his or her prayer personality.

1. **Mary.** Luke 1:46-55, Luke 2:19:

_____

_____

_____

2. **Daniel.** Daniel 6:6–11; 10:1–14:

_____

_____

_____

3. **Moses.** Exodus 32:30–32; 34:4–9:

_____

_____

_____

4. **Elijah.** 1 Kings 18:30–39:

_____

5. **Anna.** Luke 2:36–38:

6. **Nehemiah.** Nehemiah 1:4–11:

7. **Paul.** Ephesians 1:15–23; 3:14–21:

8. **David.** Psalm 25, 86, 139:

Your Prayer Assignment. Pray and choose the biblical personality most like you and your prayer strengths. After choosing a biblical person, add your unique traits to the mix. Come back prepared to share your prayer personality with the group. And then feel okay about yourself and how you pray.

Three

HOW BIG IS YOUR VISION?

After your mentor discusses praying for spiritual renewal in nations, cultures, or communities, check your understanding of the following concepts.

1. Write a definition of these spiritual events or actions.

   • Repentance:

   _____

   _____

   • Revival:

   _____

   _____

   • Spiritual awakening:

   _____

   _____

   • Transformation:

   _____

   _____

2. What are the key differences among these four definitions? To reach spiritual change, do they need to progress in a specific order?

If so, what is that order?

_____

_____

_____

_____

_____

_____

3. Write out 2 Chronicles 7:14. Circle God's requirements for true repentance. Then underline the results of that repentance.

_____

_____

_____

_____

_____

_____

4. Discuss these questions with your prayer mentoring group.

- Envision your church and how it might change through revival. What are some characteristics of a revived church? How might your church engage with your community?

_____

_____

_____

_____

_____

_____

_____

_____

- If God began to awaken the spiritually lost in your community, what evidences might you see? How could that impact your church?

_____

_____

_____

_____

_____

_____

- What if God transformed your city? Imagine and list some possible societal changes.

_____

_____

_____

_____

_____

-

- What might another Great Awakening in your nation look like?

Again, envision hopeful changes in society.

_____

_____

_____

_____

_____

_____

Your Prayer Assignment. Ask God to stir your heart for revival and spiritual awakening. Imagine how that might look in your life. Then pray for your church to be fully engaged in seeking God for a spiritual awakening that changes your community and nation.

Four

CONTENDING IN PRAYER

Think more about contending in prayer. It might be a new concept for you. Or, you might have contended and didn't know the name for it. Either way, turn your thoughts toward contending, and whether God wants you to pray in this pull-out-all-the-stops manner.

1. What is the difference between persisting and contending in prayer? See Luke 18:1-8.

_____

_____

_____

_____

_____

2. Explore some principles of contending in prayer by writing phrases from these chapters and contemplating them.

   • Increased urgency and determination. Jude 3:

_____

_____

   • Engaging in God's invitation in a cosmic battle. Daniel 10:

_____

_____

3. List other possible principles of contending in prayer. What actions might be associated with the principles you listed?

_____

_____

_____

_____

_____

4. Describe times you've fasted from food or done something else combined with prayer that might be considered contending.

_____

_____

_____

_____

_____

Your Prayer Assignment. Ask the Lord if He wants you to contend in prayer. Then ask Him for a plan. Does He want you to fast? To invite others to pray with you? Develop your plan and ask God to help you sustain it during a season of prayer. Note: If you pray about this and the Lord doesn't put anything on your heart related to contending, do not force it. A time will come when you will feel that urgency.

Five

THE POWER OF PRAYING SCRIPTURE

E.M. Bounds, a man who published much about prayer, wrote: "The study of the Word and prayer go together, and where we find the one truly practiced, the other is sure to be seen in close alliance."[7] You can create this combination by praying selected Scripture that you read and study.

1. Look up the verses below, and record how they exemplify the following reasons for praying Scripture.

   • It helps me pray when I'm not sure what to say. Acts 4:4–31:

   _____

   _____

   • It enriches the content of my prayers. Ephesians 1:15–23:

   _____

   _____

   • It focuses me on praying beyond fix-it prayers to Kingdom prayers. Luke 22:31–32:

   _____

   _____

   • It gives me a language of praise. Psalm 98 or 145:

_____

_____

- It frames how I pray for those people on my prayer list. Colossians 1:9–12:

_____

_____

- It helps me repent more. Psalm 51:

_____

_____

2. Write a personal statement about why it's beneficial to pray with Scripture.

_____

_____

_____

_____

_____

_____

Your Prayer Assignment. Practice praying The Lord's Prayer (Matthew 6:9–13), but add your own words and thoughts. Can you reframe it to make it fresh in your prayer life? Practice praying other Scripture passages as well.

Six

JESUS, THE GREATEST INTERCESSOR

Stay awake! Read Mark 14:32–42 and review the stories of Jesus and His disciples in the Garden of Gethsemane.

1. How did Jesus pray? What words in these verses describe how He prayed?

   • John 11:41–42:

   _____

   • Hebrews 5:7:

   _____

2. Review these passages and consider Jesus' invitation to ask Him for anything. What did He promise? How did He ask His followers to pray?

   • John 14:13–14:

   _____

   • John 16:24:

   _____

   • Matthew 7:7-11:

   _____

- Psalm 2:7–8:

---

3. In these passages, what was the focus of the Lord's prayers?

- Luke 6:12–13:

- Luke 22:31–32:

- Luke 23:34:

- John 17:1–24:

---

4. What does Jesus pray about now?

- Romans 8:34:

- Hebrews 7:25:

Your Prayer Assignment. This week, pray in similar ways that Jesus prayed. Practice using His examples, so you can incorporate those principles into how you intercede for others.

Seven

PAUL'S EXTRAORDINARY PRAYER LIFE

The apostle Paul modeled attitudes and principles for effective prayer in the spiritual realm. How can you pattern your outlook and requests after him?

1. Paul offered several prayer principles related to spiritual warfare. What are they?

   • Ephesians 6:10–13:

   _____

   • Ephesians 6:18–20:

   _____

   • 2 Thessalonians 3:1–2:

   _____

2. Paul prayed faithfully for all God's people, and he instructed the Church to do the same. What did he communicate about prayer in these verses?

   • 1 Thessalonians 3:10–13:

   _____

- Romans 15:5–6:

- Ephesians 1:17–21:

- 2 Thessalonians 1:11–12:

---

3. Paul let Christ shape extraordinary love in him. What was the nature of this love?

- Romans 9:1–3:

- Philippians 1:9–11:

- Ephesians 3:14–19:

---

4. Paul's thankfulness resided at the heart of his prayers: Why was he thankful?

- 1 Timothy 1:12–17:

- 1 Thessalonians 1:2–3:

- 2 Thessalonians 1:3–4:

- Colossians 1:3–4:

Your Prayer Assignment. Practice praying like Paul. Use these Scripture passages to frame your prayers related to spiritual warfare, prayer for all God's people, extraordinary love, and thankfulness. Add your words to Paul's statements.

Eight

JUST DO IT: RADICAL PRAYERS

Sometimes prayer is simply a matter of obedience, even when you don't necessarily have all that much faith. If God asks you to do it, there is a reason. So just do it!

1. When following a life of prayer, you may feel like the crazy one. But join the crowd. Let's look at some crazy, obedient people in Scripture. What did they do?

   • Joshua. Joshua 10:1–15:

   _____

   • Elijah. 1 Kings 18:20–39; 1 Kings 18:41–45:

   _____

   • Elisha. 2 Kings 6:11–18:

   _____

2. Obedience can be costly. What risk did Esther take when she prayed?

   • Esther. Esther 4:15–17; 6:1–3:

   _____

3. At times we will not understand why God asks us to do certain things, but we obey because "He says so." It's a matter of trust. How did Peter practice this principle?

   • Peter. Luke 5:1–11:

   _____

4. After reading about these people, how would you describe a radical prayer? A radical action?

   _____

   _____

   _____

   _____

   _____

   _____

Your Prayer Assignment. Ask the Lord if there is a unique way He wants you to pray. Maybe it's to take a prayerwalk or to pray boldly for healing with someone who doesn't know Christ. It could be anything, but ask the Lord if He invites you to obey outside of the ordinary. If so, do it because He said so.

Nine

BACK TO THE BASICS

Before your time with a mentoring group ends, review the basics you've learned about prayer, including your motivations and feelings about it.

1. What could be the reasons people don't pray? Circles the ones that could apply to you.

_____

_____

_____

_____

2. Now list reasons we should pray. Again, circle the reasons that apply to you.

_____

_____

_____

_____

PRAYER TAKEAWAYS

Review what you've learned about prayer during your mentoring meetings. For each of these statements, explain how the passage demonstrates what it means to your prayer life.

- Don't lose heart. Luke 18:1–8:

- Could You please just show up! 1 Kings 18:36–37:

- Nothing, nothing, nothing ... everything. 1 Kings 18:41–45:

- For survival's sake. Mark 14:34, 38; Luke 21:36:

- This is war! Daniel 10:

- Favor, plus some. Nehemiah 1:4–10; 2:4-5, 7–9:

- In a moment of panic. 2 Chronicles 20:

- This is not as good as it gets. 2 Chronicles 7:14:

Your Prayer Assignment. Note your top excuses about why you do not pray as faithfully as perhaps you should. Invite the Lord to stir a new urgency and passion in you. Ask God to make you a powerful intercessor who has Kingdom impact.

Journal

WHAT'S YOUR STORY?

In these journal pages, record your stories of answered prayer. Let them increase your hope and confidence. Keep adding to the journal and share your stories with the next generation.

JOURNAL: What's Your Story?

JOURNAL: What's Your Story?

_____

_____

_____

_____

_____

_____

_____

_____

_____

_____

_____

_____

_____

_____

_____

_____

_____

_____

_____

_____

_____

_____

_____

_____

_____

_____

End Notes

Page 27   [1]*Transformations I*, produced by Sentinel Group (*sentinel-group.org*), 2000.

Page 34   [2]Owen Murphy and John Wesley Adams, *The Fire of God's Presence* (Kansas City: Ambassadors Press, 2003), pp. 5-7.

Page 44   [3]Definition for persistence, *merriam-webster.com*. Accessed Oct. 26, 2018.

Page 45   [4]Definition for contending, *The Free Dictionary* (*thefreedictionary.com*). Accessed Oct. 26, 2018.

Page 81   [5]David Bryant. *Christ Is NOW* (New Providence, NJ: New Providence Publishers, 2017), p. 149.

Page 116   [6]Sherrie Porterfield. "Partnering with a Miracle-Working God," *Prayer Connect* magazine, Issue Five, July/August, 2012.

Page 132   [7]E.M. Bounds. *The Complete Works of E.M. Bounds* (Grand Rapids: Baker Book House, 1990), p. 326.

About the Author

Carol Madison is the editor of *PRAY* magazine and the director of prayer ministries at Hillside Church of Bloomington, MN. She also coordinates strategic prayer initiatives for PULSE, a next-generation evangelistic ministry. She operates her own business, Just Carol Editorial Resources (*justcarol.com*). Her business card says, "I write. I edit. I drink coffee. And I pray."

Carol is also a gifted teacher who can speak to your group on various aspects of prayer. Information is available at *justcarol.com*.

NATIONALDAYOFPRAYER.ORG

★ **PRAY** FOR **AMERICA** ★

THE NATIONAL DAY OF PRAYER

MOBILIZING UNIFIED
PUBLIC PRAYER
IN EVERY **TOWN**,
CITY, AND **COUNTY**
IN AMERICA

NOW PART OF THE NATIONAL
DAY OF PRAYER FAMILY!

Do you want to see a greater passion for prayer in your church?

Are you equipped to be a catalyst for prayer in your congregation?

Then you need to be a member of the

The Church Prayer Leaders Network exists to encourage, challenge, inspire, and resource you as you seek to motivate and mobilize your church toward deeper levels of prayer.

Benefits of Membership:
- Annual subscription to *PRAY* magazine
- Receive "Prayer Leader Online," a bi-monthly email that includes suggestions, inspiration and resource ideas to help you in your ministry of developing prayer.
- Discounts on prayer resources at prayershop.org

Go to prayerleader.com/membership or call 812 238-5504 to join.